Y0-DFK-092

# COMING OUT TOGETHER

# COMING OUT TOGETHER

*Memoirs on the LGBTQ+ Experience*
Edited by Shannon Ronan

OPEN AIR
PRESS

Copyright © 2023 by Shannon Ronan

All rights reserved. No part of this publication may be reproduced, stored in, or introduced into a retrieval system, or transmitted in any form or by any means (electronic, mechanical, photocopying, recording, or otherwise) without prior permission in writing from the publisher, except for the inclusion of brief quotations for a review.

First edition

Cover art and design by Breelyn MacDonald
Book design: Lawrence Tjernell and Lisa Rappoport

Printed in the United States by Versa Press, Inc.

ISBN : 979-8-218-15540-7

Open Air Press
41 Clark Street
San Rafael, CA 94901
shannon@openairpress.com

MIX
Paper from responsible sources
FSC  FSC® C005010
www.fsc.org

# Dedication

This book is dedicated to the trailblazers who came before who weathered the storms of inequality and unacceptance, and whose shoulders we stand on today. Without their strength, resiliency, and refusal to be marginalized, often at their own risk and peril, and what they endured, we would not be where we are today.

To those now taking up the torch of their predecessors' struggles, as well as their triumphs, and being brave enough to share their own stories that continue to propel us all forward towards equality, representation, and having a voice: You are a part of the fabric of progress that will give strength to future generations.

To those who read these stories and find hope within and the solace that comes from knowing you're not alone, or that it can get better, and that there is a community waiting for you on the other side; and to those who may experience the oh-so-important ability of putting yourself in someone else's shoes to expand your heart and horizons: I hope the stories within this book enable you to do that.

To Matthew Shepard: May this book do some small part in ensuring that your death wasn't in vain. That the heartbreak of having your life stolen will continue to be a catalyst for positive change. May the personal stories shared within help assist in spreading more empathy and compassion for LGBTQ+ people out into the world, with the hope that they will then help protect others from meeting the same awful fate. To prove, yet again, that love is more powerful than hate.

To Brandi and Catherine Carlile. For using your platforms and channeling your inherent characteristics of love, compassion, empathy and passion into raising marginalized voices the world over. You are both incredible beacons and examples of how to be the change we wish to see, impacting and changing lives resoundingly. Including mine. Thank you.

To the fellow misfits I have been blessed with in my own life: Thank you for making me feel supported, heard, and seen, just as I am. You know who you are.

To Amanda: For consistently having a supportive, open mind and heart when I come to you and say, "I have this idea," and for being my truth bearer by always giving me needed and honest feedback and criticism. I don't know if this book would have come to fruition without that first supportive conversation on my way home from Red Rocks that motivated me to continue with the vision for this book.

Last, but never least, to my partner in all things, Breelyn: I couldn't fathom being on this wild, beautiful, sometimes rocky, but always worth it, ride called life with anyone but you by my side. You are my balancing force and the epitome of patience, love, and staying grounded with a natural pulse on what's really important. The perpetual rebel in me is so grateful. I love you.

May the waves of progress continue to crash forward and ripple out into the world.

— Shannon Ronan

## Praise for *Coming Out Together*

"This collection weaves together the incredibly beautiful, profound, and triumphant stories of Queer existence — which in itself is an act of resiliency, resistance and joy." — Joseph Clark, Program Manager at the Oasis Center

"*Coming Out Together* is a testament to the human ability to alchemize darkness into light, over and over and over again. It will remind you that no matter who you are, you are loved." — Jane Vick, poet and writer at *Pacific Sun* newspaper

"In reading this collection of coming-out memoirs, I found myself reading my own. Though our circumstances may differ, the coming-out experience often disrupts the lives of queer folk in similar ways; in sometimes hard and necessary ways. Transformational ways. Ultimately, in ways that lead us to a life of love and peace within our truth. Tears fell as I read these words of strength and vulnerability. Each story wrapped me in community and left me with the resounding hope that together, we'll be okay. May you find yourself in these pages and may they too leave you with the realization that you are loved and you are not alone." — Amy Martin, LGBTQ+ singer/songwriter

"*Coming Out Together* is vital because it holds the hand of those who haven't yet discovered the freeing joy of crossing that threshold to find a way to live happily, practically, and lovingly." — Joe Biel, owner of Microcosm Publishing and author of *Good Trouble: Building a Successful Life & Business with Autism*

"What an exceptional example of the courage, fierceness and reality of coming out. I relived and saw pieces of me all over this book, as if someone had stolen snippets of my journal. We are all so different, yet we share the same fears that unite us in this magical, colorful, queer adventure." — Aida Kay, Host of *LGBT Chat Podcast*

# Contents

| | |
|---|---|
| Dedication | vii |
| Foreword | xiii |
| Introduction | xvii |
| Sara Bareilles "Brave" | xix |
| ADDIE KRUG   Hope Over the Rainbow | 1 |
| BOB SWITZER   All of Me | 5 |
| IDGIE   Looking Back | 13 |
| MEL FLOWERS   The Rest of the House | 21 |
| JAKE COOPER   Boy Story | 29 |
| MELISSA BARNETT   Untitled | 39 |
| KELLI NEWBY   Later | 47 |
| MICAH JAMES-ALLEN   Pieces of Light | 59 |
| LAUREN LACKEY   Diary of a Spaghetti Girl | 65 |
| KRISTEN LOOMER   Out Story | 71 |
| AVIEL McDERMOTT   The Non-Euclidean Geometry of Closet Doors | 75 |
| JANET CAMPBELL-VINCENT   Learning to Be Me | 81 |
| GEDDES FIELDER   My Coming-Out Stories | 89 |
| MILLIE   Bridging the Path | 95 |
| CARLO GOMEZ-ARTEAGA   Learning to Speak My Truth | 101 |
| LORELEI CICCONE   My Coming-Out Story | 109 |
| ANDY VINH NGUYEN   Here | 115 |
| BREELYN MACDONALD   Stages of Awakening | 121 |
| BRIAN BOWLES   Marc with a C | 131 |
| NIKKI LORTON KRUTZSCH   My Story | 143 |
| R.P. CHASE   The Beginning | 151 |
| Acknowledgments | 156 |
| Coming Out Is a Personal Journey | 158 |
| LGBTQ+ Suicide Prevention Resources | 159 |
| About Open Air Press | 161 |

# Foreword

When Shannon asked me to write the foreword to *Coming Out Together: Memoirs on the LGBTQ+ Experience,* I felt like the universe was doing something wonderfully mysterious. For the last three years I have been working on launching a nonprofit called Affirming Youth Ministries which seeks to provide safe online gathering spaces for queer youth and allies. The idea for the nonprofit was inspired by a slow waking up to how unsafe most Christian spaces are for queer folks. A small group of friends and I wanted to be part of any amount of change that could help queer youth engage their faith in environments where they would be accepted and celebrated. Since we've started, we've connected with over 600 young people from all over the world who have found community and healing in our organization. Part of this journey for me personally has been connecting with like-minded people who are also sensing a calling of sorts to spotlight and give voice to the queer experience. So, when Shannon shared her idea to put together a collection of coming-out stories, I thought it was an inspiring and serendipitous twist. I am more aware now than I've ever been of how much a book like *Coming Out Together* is needed.

After I received the advanced copy of the book, I found that I needed to read it slowly and strategically because each reflection was such a treasure of tender and profoundly personal information. Many times, I was moved to tears and needed to sit quietly and reflect or go on a walk. These are truly sacred pieces in their organic complexity and candor. As I read, it became clearer how important collections like this are in our world: collections of stories that can inspire others to be more of themselves and feel less alone, stories that have the potential to transform bigotry into love and to spark connection. These stories are at once profoundly human, yet transcendent. The writers reveal so much of the beautifully rich depth and variety residing in each human soul. And they also respect the complexity of the queer experience, adding helpful layers of nuance to what it means to be LGBTQ+.

One thing that became particularly interesting to me as I read was the variety of metaphors that people used to talk about what it was like finding out and embracing who they are. How does one describe that intimate sense of self within which will be known and experienced by the world only if it emerges? I read about how people grappled with and made sense of all the different cultural symbols that we have for gender, and how part of being queer means reinterpreting those symbols in a way that fits our individuality. The phrase "coming out" itself is also, of course, a metaphor. Each of these stories reveals our human capacity to use language to describe what it means to share ourselves with others.

Another theme that emerges in these pages is what we do with community once we have a deeper sense of who we are. In these accounts you will hear about the ending of significant relationships, broken families, healed families, churches, clubs, and so much more. One of the most significant concepts I've learned from the queer community during my work with AYM over the last three years is that of chosen family. During our life we get to choose who our family is and who we surround ourselves with and prioritize. Our family can be whoever we love and whoever loves us best.

Our students find us when most community, friends, and family have rejected them, and they are desperately seeking love and acceptance. We meet online multiple times a week and most of our students report that our community feels like a family to them. I have watched students come alive in that context. This book shows that there really is an abundance of potential family out there for all of us if we are brave enough to start looking, to start sending out the signals of our authentic selves so that the people who have the potential to love and enjoy us best can find us.

Queerness is expansion. I can't tell you how many times I've been at fundraisers with older queer people who have only the language of gay or straight to articulate their identities. They are often so intrigued by how the language and understanding around queerness keeps evolving and shifting. Because I work with young people, I feel as if I'm at the headwaters of whatever the conversation around queerness is evolving into. I've learned that this conversation isn't about gay or straight or male or female or any other sort of binary, and that there are as many expressions of identity as there are people. Kelli, one of the writers in the book, perhaps captures it best in her reflection. Upon discovering that she was queer, she writes that she "saw queerness everywhere. Not the obvious things I'd always known how to spot, but in short fingernails, an enamel pin on a collar, a tattoo, a pop culture reference. In a certain kind of eye contact."

However these stories find you, I hope you come to see that queerness is everywhere and that everything is more beautiful when we see ourselves and each other through a lens of love and affirmation. I have seen firsthand the kind of impact one simple story can have on a whole community. I am so honored to be included in this project with Shannon and can't wait to see what happens as our collective work unfolds. I know I will be spending much more time with these stories and sharing them in the various online events we host for years to come. These stories have been a deep encouragement to me, and I hope they will be for you as well.

— Scott Gronholz, Co-Director of Affirming Youth Ministries

## Introduction

It was a year ago, September 2021, when I first visited Matthew Shepard's memorial bench at the University of Wyoming on a road trip from California to see Brandi Carlile perform at Red Rocks in Colorado.

The incident in which Matthew had been beaten and left hanging for 18 hours on a fence to die, simply for being gay, happened a few months after my own coming out, and it really shook me. So when I saw I was going to be driving through the town where it had occurred, Laramie, Wyoming, I knew there had to be a memorial site in his honor I could go and visit.

Sitting on his memorial bench that day, staring at his name and the words inscribed below, was emotionally heavy for me, in a way I hadn't anticipated. After quietly ruminating there for a bit, I wiped away my tears and made a silent, firm promise to Matthew I would somehow do what I could to make sure his death wasn't in vain — that I would take his stolen life and use it as a catalyst for positive change, to somehow help others in the LGBTQ+ community. The way forward wasn't yet clear to me on this day, but the motivation certainly was. The seed was planted.

I continued on to the Brandi Carlile concert at Red Rocks, where I was surrounded by a community of people who had been brought together by music and bound by the universal, innate need to feel accepted, supported, and seen. This community, we call them The Bramily, is really a reflection of the values and goodness Brandi Carlile herself puts out into the world, and the trickle-down effect is strong.

A couple of days surrounded by that love and energy, experiencing it all with a friend who is one of the biggest pillars in my life, for both of our first times to Red Rocks, were nothing short of magical. As I began my trek back to California, I found myself in a space of quiet reflection, looking out at the beautiful scenery of the Rocky

Mountains, when a light bulb went off. In this community of people I was blessed to be a part of, I had shared, and heard, a number of coming-out stories. Some hard, some ugly, some good. But all important.

I thought, what if I gather as many coming-out stories as I can and put them together to share with the world, in the hopes that this sharing would help others going through the process of coming out to know that they're not alone, or that it can get better, or that it might just not be all that bad? And it would help create empathy for those who read these stories as well: healing for both authors and readers. I know, I'll start a publishing company centered around illuminating marginalized voices, and call it Open Air Press, symbolic of these voices being released into the world. And I'll donate a percentage of proceeds from this book back to The Matthew Shepard Foundation as well as the Looking Out Foundation to help them further their important work. The seed had taken roots.

May this book lend a hand and voice in contributing to the positive ripple effects of progress.

— Shannon Ronan

## "Brave" by Sara Bareilles

*You can be amazing*
*You can turn a phrase into a weapon or a drug*
*You can be the outcast*
*Or be the backlash of somebody's lack of love*
*Or you can start speaking up*
*Nothing's gonna hurt you the way that words do*
*When they settle 'neath your skin*
*Kept on the inside and no sunlight*
*Sometimes a shadow wins*
*But I wonder what would happen if you*
*Say what you wanna say*
*And let the words fall out*
*Honestly I wanna see you be brave*
*With what you want to say*
*And let the words fall out*
*Honestly I wanna see you be brave*
*I wanna see you be brave*
*I just wanna see you*
*I wanna see you be brave*
*Everybody's been there, everybody's been stared down*
*By the enemy*
*Fallen for the fear and done some disappearing*
*Bow down to the mighty*
*But don't run, stop holding your tongue*
*Maybe there's a way out of the cage where you live*
*Maybe one of these days you can let the light in*
*Show me how big your brave is*
*Say what you wanna say*
*And let the words fall out*
*Honestly I wanna see you be brave*
*With what you want to say*
*And let the words fall out*
*Honestly I wanna see you be brave*
*Innocence, your history of silence*
*Won't do you any good*
*Did you think it would?*
*Let your words be anything but empty*
*Why don't you tell them the truth?*
*Say what you wanna say*
*And let the words fall out*
*Honestly I wanna see you be brave*
*With what you want to say*
*And let the words fall out*
*Honestly I wanna see you be brave*
*I wanna see you be brave*
*See you be brave*

## Addie Krug ❖ Hope Over the Rainbow

I've learned that there is a life-saving power in loving everyone. I've learned to allow my courage to outdistance my fear so I can fully embrace what the world brings me. I've learned that my truth can be lived if I pulverize the walls of shame standing between two versions of myself. Without coming out, I wouldn't have learned these lessons. I was offered a new hope and perspective on life when I began celebrating who I am, rather than walking in secrecy. I have cultivated new relationships, found communities that feel like families, and been able to use my insight to help others, which is the greatest gift in the world.

Coming out is hard, and those who haven't taken that step are still valid and loved beyond measure. For me, it was hard to realize this. I repeated to myself that doubt and confusion automatically meant I was lying to myself. My biggest fear when anticipating coming out was that I would no longer belong to or experience community, which was made true in the best way possible. I felt very unaccepted by organizations I once proudly supported; coming out served as a gateway to being a part of something more loving. Doors closed on me, and better ones opened. Community has given me the chance to hear other people's stories and experiences in discovering themselves and finding the pure comfort of understanding I'm not alone.

I believe that as people, we are all made to reflect different beams of light and love to those around us. We all have a beautiful story, unique to us, and every story matters in the eternal unfolding of loving bigger and affirming better. Our stories turn into our possibility to influence the people around us. We discover our destinies through our personal experiences. Coming out could give so many people a pathway to helping others fully embrace who they are.

*Strength comes from living your truth. To be true and authentic is your path to happiness, peace, and joy.*
— Anonymous

*Sheryl,*

*You are an amazing light in this world. I hope you enjoy this book and the light from the authors within. I'M AN AUTHOR!! Thank you for being an ally!*

*♥ - B*

## Bob Switzer ❖ All of Me

The day I decided to be all of me was terrifying. Is there a stronger word than that for fear? If there is, I was that. I had hidden who I was for so long that I had to hurt people to share all of me with them. I was married for 27 years to a wonderful woman, and we raised two incredible children who are, as I write this, 21 and 23 years old. How am I supposed to tell the woman that I have built such a strong life with that I'm gay? Oh, and also, over our thirty-year relationship, there were times when I was being me where I was not faithful to you, but don't worry, I was being safe. For those of you like me, you know how it feels to try and rationalize that since we are not cheating with women it makes it better somehow, so we can live with what we are doing instead of killing ourselves. It doesn't, but I get it.

I knew it was important to tell her everything. I couldn't just say, "I'm gay. Sorry. No questions please. Now I'm going to go do gay stuff." I had to tell her the whole truth and focus on how my being gay had nothing to do with her. I did not try to use other failures in our marriage to soften the blow or take away from that fact. I don't remember how many times I silenced the television that morning before I finally hit mute one last time and croaked that I had to tell her something. But still the words would not come out. My eyes filled with tears. I was going to destroy this woman's life with two words.

She grabbed my hands and held them as I struggled to speak. I choked and finally let the words go.

"I'm gay."

After she cried with me and tried to comfort me, she said that she would help me continue to hide by staying married to me. I kindly made it clear that I was not interested in hiding anything anymore. I was tired of the lies and tired of hiding ... exhausted actually. That reaction from her, though, helped me start the conversation in helping her to see how I was able to love her for all those years while being gay. From the outside, we looked like we had a perfect marriage and, even though it wasn't, it was pretty damn great. Over the years we had both become so comfortable and complacent in our marriage that we were adept at the everyday ins and outs of a relationship even though the intimate part of it had been dormant for many years. I think we can all agree that love is much more than just sexual attraction. I did not want to be gay and if you really are gay, then you know there is nothing you can do about it. I prayed. I pushed it down hoping it would go away. I tried to fuck the gay away with women. I got married hoping for a "normal life." I tried. Hard. Still gay.

I could go on and on about how I know that being who you are is not a choice, but there are important details of my story that you need to know because, as hard as it is, just saying the words is not enough.

I shared with her how it feels to be me, and unburdened myself of the secrets and lies that had weighed me down for years. In between one of the awkward silences, we decided that the next step was telling our children. We did that together the next day. I think it helped for the kids to see us being a united front as she sat silently holding my hand while I told them their dad was a less fabulous version of Elton John. I received support and love from them too, even if they didn't fully understand everything. I think that was because I was even better at being a father than I was at being a husband, and we had raised our kids to be accepting, tolerant, and caring of different kinds of people.

Over the next week my wife and I went on my "Coming-Out Tour." We told the important members of our family, our friends, and other people close to us. I even sent an email to almost all my co-workers, which I prefaced with an apology about how an email was probably not the best way to tell them. Most people were confused but supportive, and the ones who were not had valid reasons for being angry with me because they believed I had stolen so many years of her life by not being honest. She assured them that was not true even if she was not fully convinced that it wasn't. I know that she had her doubts because in between stops on the tour, we drove around for hours and talked and cried. Sometimes I even had to pull into a parking lot so we could talk louder and cry harder, because it is incredibly difficult to drive while trying to make sense of how we were going to be okay.

She asked the questions most people do, like when did I first know I was gay and why did I wait so long to come out. She already knew how tough my childhood was, and so it was easy to answer most of them. My mom and dad struggled with substance abuse; their marriage lasted nine years before they divorced. My mother started dating our neighbor. He was even more of a drunk than my biological parents combined, and my mother followed him happily downward into darkness. They beat my sister and me with whatever was closest. My sister and I had only curtains as doors, but we would stay "jailed" in our rooms for months except to do chores, go to school and eat meals (that we usually prepared ourselves), because solitary confinement was better than the alternative. We ran away three times in as many years, but the police always brought us back. It wasn't until I found out that my stepfather was doing something far worse to my sister that I set fire to the house so the police would have nowhere to bring us back to. The truth came out after the fire, and my sister and I ended up in separate foster homes until we graduated from high school.

I was living with my second foster family when I started to realize that I was gay. I remember trying to come to terms with it and thinking, "Are you fucking kidding me? After all of that terrible shit I'm gay too?!"

Thus began my fight to hide it forever. Like I said before, I did not want to be it. Sure, there were times when life was going well where the big gay monster inside of me was reduced to a low growl. But it was those times when I was just minding my own business and definitely not being gay, while definitely being gay, when I would see someone or something that would make me feel something that was definitely gay. That feeling was just as scary as it was exciting. I would immediately try to distract myself and hope that no one could read my body language or see the glimmer in my eyes and discover that my big gay monster did not like being locked up.

When my monster roared it sounded something like this:

*"I want to stroke that man's beard, feel his touch, fall into him and be held in those big, strong, hairy, muscular arms."*

*"Did he just see me look down at his bulge? Was he looking at mine?!"*

*"I'm going to touch it. He wants me to touch it. I'm not going to touch it. Oh shit, I touched it. I have to stop touching it! It feels so good to touch it! Now touch mine!"*

And let's not leave out the few times I secretly watched *Brokeback Mountain* and yearned to have that connection with another man, and how "I wish I knew how to quit you" hits a lot harder when you have the same secret.

One of my final moments of hiding myself happened while watching *Queer Eye* and realizing that maybe I could find the courage to let my big gay monster loose once and for all:

*"Did my wife just see me relating way too much and choking back tears about that pastor who came out later in life and how the Fab Five helped him realize all of himself while repairing his church, throwing away all of his cargo shorts, and French-tucking his shirts? Then those other gay clergy people showed up to champion him into being proud of who he was and empowered him to lead all kinds of people into their own journey of self-acceptance?"*

It was a few days later that I got the courage to say the words to my wife, but she was not the first person I shared it with. A few weeks before I saw that episode of *Queer Eye* I met a guy. It was not, and was, as complicated as you think. I did not go out looking for him. He was not looking for me either. We did find each other though.

I was out walking because Covid-19 was still keeping the gyms closed and it was a nice break from running in place on the elliptical and being quarantined to the house. He was out doing the same. We made eye contact while passing each other. I saw him see me. The real me. I recognized that knowing gaze, and I turned to look at him again. He did too. I thought it was going to be like the other times that I gave in to my big gay monster and then went back to being the normal, straight husband and father of two for which I was so well known. But then we started to talk. I poured my heart out and he listened. He shared with me that he had hidden for a long time too and told me his story, which included a husband who had passed away, much too young, after battling cancer; that made me realize that life is too short to not be all of who I am.

I found out that he knew people who knew me, and I was terrified that he would destroy my entire life. The more we talked, though, I realized that I had nothing to fear from him and that my sexuality was about a lot more than just sex. I wanted to go out to dinner with a guy, watch television with a guy, go to the grocery store with a guy, argue over ridiculous things with a guy, and be with a guy as if it were just as normal as straight people are allowed to be, without ridicule. At this point I did not know if this guy was the actual guy that I wanted to do all of those things with, but he was willing to let me in and listen to me and, dammit, did it feel good to talk about being gay. The day before I said the words to my wife, he told me that he was going camping for the weekend and made me promise that I would wait to tell anyone until I was able to talk to him again so we could figure it out together. He could sense that I was scared to death but very close to being strong enough to do it. I promised him that

I would. I didn't though. That next morning is when I pressed that mute button on the remote one last time and unmuted myself. That was five months ago.

My wife and I tried to maintain some semblance of a normal life and continued to live together in the same house. We talked about getting a duplex so our eventual separate lives would be less separate. After about a week or so, though, it became harder to live under the same roof and not be the same married couple that we were before. I told her about my concerns with our duplex idea being too hard for both of us, and that I felt that if we lived together any longer our relationship could get toxic. Neither of us wanted to hate the other. So, the guy I met welcomed me into his home and gave me a room to stay in while I waited a month for my apartment to be available. I continued to make my family a priority while the guy helped me figure out what it meant to be all of me.

I have been writing this over the last two nights while he and I are on a weekend getaway. He is snoring right now while I type this sentence because it is 2:30 AM on Sunday morning, October 11th, 2020. Ironically and wonderfully, today is National Coming-Out Day. In the last five months I have worked hard to keep my wife and children in my life. They are working hard to keep me in their lives too. We do not have it all figured out yet, but we have done a lot of healing and recognize that we still have a long road ahead of us. We are separated but not divorced. We have dubbed our relationship "the unicorn" as a colorful way to describe to others how we still love each other and plan to stay close as a family for the rest of our lives. "The guy" and I have worked hard on figuring out how he will fit into our lives as well. They have all met him now because it turns out that he has the potential to be the guy that I want to do all of the normal everyday stuff in life with, and all of the normal gay stuff with too.

Your situation is probably different from mine and holds other seemingly insurmountable obstacles. Surmount them. You might not be able to hold on to your family like I have. You might lose other people who are close to you now, at least in the beginning. I went all-in that morning, fully expecting to be hated, and risked losing them forever. I was ready either way. I was tired of lying to everyone and myself. Make sure you have a plan for a safe place to stay and people strong enough to emotionally support you through any outcome of your coming out. Get counseling and surround yourself with people who love you. Believe me, once you remove that weight from your shoulders you will start to feel better. I still struggle sometimes, but it's only because I care about keeping all these people in my life and I worry that I am never doing enough. The guilt of moving on after loving and building a life with someone for 30 years is still overwhelming too. I am so sorry I can't be there to help you through your journey and remind you that it will get better and that you will be okay. Good luck, my friend. All these words were written for you. I hope it helps.

## Idgie ❖ Looking Back

Why is it that some things are so much clearer in hindsight? I guess that's just how it works. When you're in a moment, in a certain time and place, meeting a certain person, how can you possibly know the profound ripple effect that person will have on you and your life?

When I met my future first girlfriend, it was on a softball field (cue the lesbian jokes), and I was 14 years old. Being the natural social butterfly I was, I distinctly remember walking up to the girl I'd never been on a prior team with and saying, "Hi. I'm Idgie. What's your name?" The curiosity and intrigue were instant. Maybe it was because in a small town, meeting someone new was pretty rare. Or was it the way she spoke and how her green, almond-shaped eyes made prolonged direct contact that threw me? Regardless, I was happy to have her on the team (no pun intended).

Soon enough, after numerous practices and games, traveling to different towns, sharing laughs and conversations, we became inseparable. It wasn't long before I was spending most weekends at her house, staying up late into the night getting to know each other, and bonding in a way reserved for those years as a carefree teenager. Looking back, I was blissed out and having those happiness butterflies that, frankly, only happen when the feelings for someone expand beyond "friends." Those were some of the happiest times of my life — if I could freeze-frame it to the first year of becoming friends, and then the beginnings of being more. But I don't want to get ahead of myself.

Cut to the next summer, when we happily found ourselves on another softball team together. I was now 15, and only a couple of days away from 16. I'll always distinctly remember that sweet grass smell of summer that filled her bedroom, and the chorus of crickets that filled the air.

We were, as usual, lying in bed with the warm summer breeze hitting our skin as we lay talking and laughing. The musical likes of The Sundays and Mazzy Star filled the air. At this point we had recently taken to giving each other massages. Meaning, we would swap lying on top of each other, massaging the other's back and shoulders. Yes, lying on top of each other. Again, looking back, the things that become clear. I know now I don't normally lie on top of my "friends" while they massage me. But I was definitely not objecting at the time.

Things must have occurred to her before they did to me, because soon enough we found ourselves yet again in this position, with me massaging her back. Then I started to feel her lips softly kissing and making their way up my neck. My entire body went from happily tingly (perhaps another sign of my propensity to things "lesbian") to instantly stiff and frozen. I don't think I really had time to register what was happening until her lips got right to mine...and then I turned my head.

The next thing I remember was running after her down the road, trying to reassure her that I wasn't mad, everything was okay. Then just sitting 10 feet apart on the hill in silence, both of us scared and so confused — looking back, most likely for reasons more similar than not. At the time, she must have felt more alone in her newfound gay leanings, as I wasn't quite ready to explore what was so obvious yet. I always felt bad about that — I left her hanging when she had finally built up the courage to make the first move on another female. She was braver than me in this moment and regard. I just wasn't ready yet…at least not for, oh, a week or so. I guess some could say it was a pretty quick gay U-turn. Or the right turn, but I just had to wait for when it felt right for me to advance.

While we didn't take a break from spending time together, nor my spending weekends at her house, we did develop an invisible barrier between us when going to bed. If one's foot should accidentally graze the other's, there was an overcompensating lightning-fast pull-back to show just how much anything more than friendship wasn't on the table (usually reserved for when people know full well there is more than friendship on the table).

Cut to a few days later, and our bodies slowly began migrating back towards each other. First to cuddle as we slept, then soon enough, the good ol' massages kicked back in. However, this time, I'd had some time to think on things. As my hands made their way down to her lower back, I pulled her closer and flipped us, so we were facing each other on our sides, using one hand to hold the side of her face to have her look me in the eye, briefly, before kissing her. It felt all sorts of intense, and right.

The next few months were full of all that elated, walking on sunshine, unbridled happiness that comes with first love, or the sweet beginnings of any relationship, for that matter. However, societal stigma was definitely alive and well. It was 1996, and in the small mountain town I grew up in, there were no other examples of gay people around. Not even one that I knew — at least not any that were "out." Not to mention, while my family weren't regularly practicing Catholics (meaning, I have very few memories of conversations relating to our lives and choices being driven by "what would Jesus do," and even fewer of actually going to church outside of some holidays growing up), my Mom and aunts did grow up going to Catholic girls' school, and it was an unspoken thing that these were our family's inherent beliefs. Due to this, I distinctly remember walking down the hallways of high school, all blissed out, but every once in a while, I'd feel this huge dread of guilt that would kick me in the emotional gut. I remember thinking to myself, what's wrong with me? Am I going to hell? How could something that feels so natural and right be a sin? It was a very confusing, lonely time, let alone being 16 and navigating the complexities of high school.

For the next two years I remained firmly in the closet. My friends basically thought I was a secretive, serial maker-outer, as I'd sometimes, ahem, have hickeys adorning my neck once Monday rolled back around. I'd explain them away as, oh that was from this random guy I met at so and so's. They'd all laugh and give me shit and move on. Whew. Saved again. This got harder as time went on, though. Not only because I hated lying to them, but also because I hated having to hide. And a lot of the time we were all together during the weekends, so I imagine it confused them where I made the time. Though, looking back, maybe I wasn't as sly as I thought, and I just had amazing people in my life that didn't care. But I'll get to that.

The thing is, hiding yourself from those you love can end up taking a toll. It can eat at you, and make you feel like you're this insincere person who can never truly be wholly themselves, when that's really all you want — to be wholly yourself. Throw in the guilt, as is built in societally, as well as religiously, around being gay, and it's something that's bound to bubble over. The hope is that when it does, you will have the support system there that embraces all of you. Not everyone is so lucky, but I was.

My first "bubble over" moment was with one of my best friends. We took a walk to a local park near my house and sat down on some steps. I don't remember planning to come out on this particular day or place, but sometimes when the moment strikes…

As soon as I'd made the decision to spill my gay guts out, I started shaking and crying — so much pent-up emotion and adrenaline hit me all at once. I was so scared. She put her arm around me and declared, "You know you can tell me anything, it won't change anything." So, I took a huge breath and told her everything. How for 2+ years I'd been involved as more than friends with she-who-won't-be-named, why the attachment there had always seemed a little much, how it started, how hard it had been. She listened, and at the end said, "Well duh. I pretty much already had a good idea this was going on. I just don't care; it doesn't affect our friendship or how much I love you in the slightest." It was like she was waiting for me to share my truth.

Cue the floodgates. Partly due to relief, partly due to feeling wholly seen for the first time. I truly believe this was one of those life-altering moments that can take your hand and direct you towards becoming who you are meant to be, or drive you further into the proverbial closet of fear and guilt. It scares me to think about where I would have ended up had I not been blessed with this acceptance. Over the next couple of weeks, I found the courage to have the come-out conversation with a few of my other close friends, who were also not surprised, but most importantly, also didn't care. They loved me for me, not for who or what I was doing in the bedroom. The compound effects of this on my life are incalculable, as are the levels of gratitude.

Coming out on a societal level continues to be an ongoing process, from being hyper-aware in certain settings of the judgmental looks while holding hands walking down the street, or kissing in public on a date, to spending time with family members who haven't worked out the cognitive dissonance of their own beliefs and personal feelings matching up within. 25 years later, after sitting on those park steps with a dear friend and taking that leap of exposing my lady-loving ways, I can happily say I have found myself blessed with a relationship of 18+ years thus far with the most amazing, loving, grounded force of nature of a Woman anyone can hope to know, let alone share their life with. I hope you are in the position and place to take the leap when you're ready. You just can't know what kind of acceptance, community, and love might be waiting on the other side.

Hope is the thing with feathers –
That perches in the soul –
And sings the tune without the words –
And never stops – at all –

– Emily Dickinson

## Mel Flowers ❖ The Rest of the House

The term "coming out" means something different to everyone. Some people think of it as a singular pivotal moment in their life and can pinpoint it to one singular event. Whether that be when they told their mom and dad through tears one day after a hard day of junior high school, or telling the extended family over Thanksgiving dinner while home on break from college, they have one occasion their mind jumps to when asked about their coming-out story.

To me, coming out is something I must do on the regular. As queer people, we are coming out more often than we think we are. For example, when I am at the hardware store looking to make a big purchase and I tell the salesperson that I will have to think it over and come back, I'm sometimes met with, "Sure, no problem. Go home and talk it over with your husband and let us know." When I was younger, this kind of statement would make me incredibly uncomfortable, and I would just agree and beat myself up on the way back home. If that were to happen today, I would meet the employee's statement with my truth by telling him that I will be sure to talk it over with my wife and come back when we decide. In this instance, I feel that my "coming out" was more for that employee than it was for me. Maybe next time, they will think twice about making assumptions about a customer's orientation. This kind of thing needs to be normalized, and we can help make that happen by having interactions such as this. The older I get, the less I think about my response.

As a musician, coming out happens in a different way. After playing a show, there's always some drunk guy willing to make an ass out of himself in front of his friends after your set. "Hey baby, can I buy you a drink?" "You're great for a girl, can I get your number?" "You want to get out of here when you put your guitar away?" While flattering, this was always tricky territory. I know when answering I'll be met with either support, kindness, perversion, or disgust. I used to come up with an excuse about "my boyfriend." That would usually put an end to things very quickly. I was afraid of what their response would be if I told the truth: that my girlfriend was on the other side of the bar getting drinks, or in the bathroom, or at work. As queer people, it is inevitable that we will be met with resistance and rejection. Take back the power of that interaction and realize the other person's response is a reflection of them and who they are, and not a reflection of who you are. While these daily and sometimes insignificant "coming outs" take up some space in my memory bank, there are also those pivotal and permanent memories that were far more eventful and life-changing.

When I was in kindergarten, I was obsessed with one of my classmates. She had the most beautiful long brown hair and eyes that glittered against that playground backdrop. When I told the teacher at my private Christian school that I wanted her to be my girlfriend, my teacher laughed and said, "Girls don't have girlfriends. Girls have boyfriends." In reality, I was coming out to my teacher in a roundabout way before I even knew what being gay or coming out was. This was the start of my religious trauma that would haunt me a majority of my life.

I was raised by a Catholic dad and a Southern Baptist mom and grandmother. It was always just the four of us in the house and as the only child, I was often the center of attention. This made me want to never disappoint my family. With all our extended family in the sticks of Kentucky, I was all they had to focus on in rural Illinois when it came to family. This put a lot of pressure on me to be everything they wanted me to be.

I tried my best to be a "good Christian" and follow their rules. I even had my fair share of middle school and junior high boyfriends (most of whom later turned out to be gay themselves). When I reached high school, I left my private religious junior high school and was enrolled in a high school down the road that even had the word "Christian" in the name. I was looking forward to being a freshman, making new friends, and experiencing new things. Little did I know, those new things would land me in a whole heap of trouble.

She had beautiful black dyed hair and an adorable way of pushing her glasses up on her nose. Like myself, she was big into music and introduced me to countless new bands. I knew that our friendship was developing into something different. She was a senior and I was a freshman. She had come out to our friend group in the years before I entered the school. She was the first out gay person I had ever met, and I was fascinated.

After a few months of flirting, she finally officially asked me out. I couldn't contain myself. I told everyone in our group of friends immediately. We had been going out for a couple of weeks, and everything was perfect.... Until one day, the choir teacher found us in the band room closet together. Yes, I do understand the irony of the situation. We weren't doing anything naughty, but we were probably closer together than friends should be. Needless to say, we were sent immediately to the very Christian principal's office at the end of the hall of the very Christian school.

When my mom picked me up that day, the situation was explained to her. She blamed it on peer pressure and outside influences. The next day, after dinner, I finally worked up the courage to tell her what was really going on. The conversation went something like this:

"Mom, I have something to tell you."

"What is it, honey?"

"That thing that happened at school was more than you thought it was. That girl and I are dating. She's my girlfriend. I'm gay." Silence.

"I'd rather be dead than have a gay daughter."

The painful revelation of my mother's true feelings and those nine words that cut through me like a knife played over and over in my head the next few days. I couldn't believe I'd hurt my mom that badly. I felt like I had completely let her down. It was an only child's worst nightmare. My mom wasn't feeling much better than I was. She couldn't stop crying. I had completely torn her apart.

I moved out of the house on my 18th birthday and in with my much older and very new girlfriend. Much to my mother's dismay, our communication was limited to only necessary correspondences. That relationship lasted about five years. It wasn't the best situation. My mom knew that. I will never know if it was just mother's intuition or if I'd accidentally pocket-dialed her during one of our more extreme arguments. This felt like another strike against my sexuality, another reason for my mom to hate "the gays."

My mom's dream came true when I became pregnant after not wanting to let her down, and forcing myself to be with a man I didn't truly love. I tried to convince myself I loved him. I wanted to love him for the sake of my family. I wanted to see my mother's eyes light up when I brought him to holidays. I wanted to have a bond with her where we both talked about our significant others: the annoying things they do, and how we secretly loved those things. I had never had that with her. There was an unspoken rule that I didn't speak of my same-sex partners. Around her, I had to pretend they didn't exist.

As with a lot of traditional Southern Baptist families, with baby comes marriage. I was engaged to marry a person of the wrong sex I didn't even love. I did it for her. I did it for the mother who would rather be dead than want me to be myself. I did it to dry her tears and make her proud of me again. I cried on my wedding day. These were not the tears that matrimony usually brings. They were tears of great sorrow and loss. I lost myself that day. It felt like I was giving up my soul and being sworn to secrecy about my true identity.

You guessed it. The marriage lasted about as long as an ice cube in hell. I couldn't do it anymore. I couldn't lie to myself and everyone around me. The moment this really clicked with me was one morning when I was looking at my daughter. Not only had I married an irresponsible and controlling alcoholic, but I had married into a lie and a charade. How could I ever tell my sweet little daughter to be herself always no matter the consequences if I wasn't practicing what I preached?

My mom took the news of the divorce much better than I thought she would. I think she realized how toxic an environment it was for my little girl, who had become the apple of her eye. The news she didn't take as well came a few months later.

I had met the love of my life long before I married someone I didn't love. I saw her as soon as she walked into the room. She came to see my band perform at a Halloween show at a local venue. It turned out we had mutual friends through some of my bandmates. She introduced herself to me and when she walked away, I told the singer of my band I was going to marry that girl one day. I was with a guy I didn't like. The best part was she was also with a guy she didn't like. I thought of her on my wedding day. Some of those tears I cried were for her.

The love of my life and I never had any type of relationship until we were both separated from our significant others. I had left my drunk husband on the side of the road and sent him divorce papers the next day. She had caught her boyfriend cheating with the woman who lived across the street from them. Both of those stories sound so unfortunate, but really, it was just the stars making a mess in order to align.

The news of her breakup came from a mutual friend at another show I was playing. My friend was talking to her on the phone. I grabbed the phone and told her she had to come to the show. It was very important to me that she be there. She pulled into the parking lot about 30 minutes after hanging up.

After that show, we grabbed dinner a few times and hung out as friends. I invited her to another show my band was playing in town. I got there way earlier than our suggested load-in time, just to anticipate her arrival. I saw her walking up to the venue....with a date. I was completely crushed. I could have sunk into that venue's sticky wooden floor. I thought it was going to be the night I professed my love, but it seemed as though someone had beaten me to the punch. I couldn't help but be short with her the rest of the night. She got me alone and asked what was wrong. I told her I was upset because I was jealous. When she asked why, I stumbled over every thought and blurted, "Because I have a crush on you, dude." She stopped and replied, "I have a crush on you too." My heart did the opposite of sink. It rose to the heavens. We kissed for the first time, over a year after our first meeting. It was everything I wanted that moment to be. Three years later, we have hardly spent a day without each other.

What does this have to do with coming out, you ask? Well, I wanted to show you how beautiful my love is. Love like that shouldn't be hidden. It should be displayed proudly for everyone to see. If you have a love like that, you shouldn't be ashamed. You shouldn't feel like you can't show the world. There will always be those who disapprove. Love is stronger than hate. Loving out loud can inspire, educate, and warm the hearts of those around us.

While I'm still coming out every day in little ways to strangers and acquaintances, the last big milestone coming-out event was, again, with my mother. My current partner and I had been dating for about three months. I was tired of keeping her a secret and wanted to share our love with the world. I had to start with my strongest adversary.

One day, as I was running out the door in a hurry, I looked at my mom and said, "By the way, I've been dating someone new. It's a girl. She's coming over for dinner tomorrow."

Of course, my mom didn't go from wanting to die to head of the queer welcoming committee overnight. The first introduction and subsequent visits were awkward and even cold at times. Fast-forward three years, my partner and I see my mom several times a week. In fact, my mom has been trying to get out of me what my partner wants the most for Christmas so she can buy it before me. She loves her and views her as a part of the family. For this, I will be eternally grateful.

Those big important coming-out moments are always hard, regardless of how you think the news will be received. I just want you to know you never have to be ashamed of being yourself. If someone truly loves you, they will accept you. It may take time, but patience is rewarding. If you feel rejected by some, remember there are those who will always love you for you. I love you and your true authentic self. You don't have to come out today, or even tomorrow or next week. You will know when the moment feels right to open that closet door and finally stand on the other side. The rest of the house is way nicer than the closet.

### Jake Cooper ❖ Boy Story

For better or for worse, I am a member of Generation X, through and through. Meaning, all of my childhood memories are associated with toys, cartoons, and McDonald's, or commercials for toys, cartoons, and McDonald's.

An essential day in any boy's life is when he gets a Barbie Doll of his very own. Correction, an important day in this boy's life was when he got a Barbie Doll of his very own. I recall vividly the day my mom agreed to buy me my own Barbie. As a young child, I played with my sisters' Barbies all the time. However, they were my sisters' Barbies, not mine, and by the time I was nine, my sisters outgrew them. They had all received bad lesbian haircuts or were amputees of some kind, so my mom decided to toss them.

My mother and I were having lunch at our special place, a coffee shop in the mall that made me feel very fancy because I could get a club sandwich. Also, they served chips instead of fries, and you got a pickle spear. It was that pickle spear that made it classy. But I digress. Mom and I were eating lunch there one day; I was nine or ten. The toy store was next to the café in the mall.

"Mom, can I go to Thornberry's and get a toy?"

"Maybe, what is it you want?"

I was very into He-Man figures at this time. No big surprise that they were my favorite toys, heavily muscled men wearing fur panties. Even the villain Skeletor had rock-hard pecs and thighs that could crack walnuts. But on that day, I didn't want a He-Man figure. What I wanted was Day-to-Night Barbie: corporate eighties yuppie by day, jetsetting fashion plate by night. I had become fixated on Day-to-Night Barbie ever since I saw her reversible ensemble in the TV commercial that aired regularly during Saturday morning cartoons.

"I want... well, I want... umm...."

"What is it, Boy?"

Something in her green eyes gave me the slightest feeling my mother was bracing herself.

"You can tell me anything."

"Well... I want a Barbie." I said."I just want to fix its hair and stuff, but never mind can I get a new He-Man?"

She did not miss a beat. "You can get a Barbie if you want one. There is nothing wrong with being creative. But if you want this to be our secret, that's OK, Boy."

Boy. It is ironic that I would be identified by a word I have yet fully to identify with. What does it mean to be a boy? I was born on June 29th, 1975, in Louisville, Kentucky. As a city, Louisville has what I would consider a case of multiple personality disorder. Called "the gateway to the South," Louisville has the welcoming friendliness of a big southern town, with the arts and culture of a thriving metropolis. We also have a pretty famous horse race here every year in May.

I grew up in a typical American neighborhood, in a typical American tri-level house resplendent with orange shag carpet, furniture made from barrels and covered in tanned leather, velveteen throw pillows, and wood paneling in the basement. This was a predominantly Catholic neighborhood. There were four different parishes all within walking distance of our house. This was a neighborhood where every kid knew each other, where lawns were full of bicycles and driveways were covered in chalk. Where cardinals made their nests in oak trees that dropped so many acorns, we made a game of running across them barefoot. A neighborhood with summers hot enough to run through the sprinklers in the front yards and winters cold enough to freeze the water in the small ditch that ran through the back yards. There were trees to climb, and sidewalks to ride bikes on, and yards big enough for massive games of frozen catchers. I knew every crack in the sidewalk, I knew every bush to hide behind, I knew exactly how long it took to walk to the Convenient mini-mart to buy Now & Laters and exactly which yards to cut through. This was the world I grew up in; however, it was never a world in which I truly belonged. I am so glad I didn't know that then.

I was named Jason Gregory after my dad, but he goes by Greg, which maybe signified at birth how fundamentally different he and I were going to be. I am one of those people on whom many a nickname has been bestowed. My large extended family calls me "Jake" after my late grandfather, who was the first Jason. My nieces and nephews have branded me "Bubba," which is mortifying when spoken in public. In school, people mostly called me "Cooper," which seems to be one of those last names that serves as a single moniker amongst friends and aggressive female PE teachers. Sometimes "Cooper" is shortened to "Coop" because, apparently, if people like you, they want to use only one syllable. Once, after getting a bad bowl haircut, my sister Rebecca started referring to me as "Dot," implying that I looked like champion figure skater Dorothy Hamill with her trademark wedge. However, most of my life, likely because I have three older sisters, my family has simply referred to me as Boy.

"Where's Boy?"

"This is for Boy."

"What is Boy doing?"

In all honesty, I was probably about thirteen before I truly realized I was a boy and should perhaps at least pretend to act like one. During the first five or six years of my life, I wore pajama bottoms on my head to mimic my sisters' long hair. Those were happy years playing house, learning how to ride a bike, learning how to roller skate. There is quite a bit of photographic evidence of me engaging in these childhood rites of passage. The pajama bottoms are in their rightful place on my head.

Being the youngest and only son following three daughters, I was born with expectations thrust upon me. "The day you were born was the happiest day of my life." Every year on my birthday, my mother tells me this. She says it was the most content she ever was in her life. She says that for a moment, life was perfect.

Why wouldn't it have been? She had a hardworking husband, three beautiful little girls, and finally, the answer to my parents' prayers, a perfect baby boy. Little did she know that the perfect baby boy would rebel almost instantly against that title.

I was at the park. I was eight or nine years old, and some kid came up to me and barked, "What are you?"

I knew immediately that this was the kind of fellow child I tried to avoid. As a kid I felt somewhat cautious around those I thought were a little red around the neck. I am from Kentucky; I am allowed to say that.

"What do you mean?" I asked, trying not to sound defensive or, worse, scared.

"Are you a boy or a girl?" he said, his voice laced with eight-year-old malice.

"I'm a boy, you idiot," I snapped.

Despite my false bravado, I was upset. I had been asked this question before quite often, even by my cousin Annie who had a mullet and wore a football jersey to Christmas dinner.

"Why did he ask me that?" I asked my mother later that day.

"Probably because you are so handsome, you are almost as pretty as a girl," she said with a matter-of-fact smile that seemed to give me permission to dismiss the incident.

Well, that takes care of that. The kid at the playground inquired about my gender because I was so good-looking. I suppose the fact that I was pretending to be Olivia Newton-John while reënacting Xanadu on the swing set had nothing at all to do with it.

Ah, Olivia, I love her. I had all her records. The highlight of any second grader's life has to be the day he got the 45 of "Physical." On any given day, I could usually be found in our family room stacking 45s on the turntable of our stereo, the type of stereo that looks like a liquor cabinet with a speaker on the side. I think this model of stereo was mandatory for every household in the 1970s. I can still hear the clicking sound of the needle retracting as the next record dropped. The next record was almost always "Dancing Queen."

I was forged by the fires of disco. I was singing along to disco records before I could put sentences together. Some of my first utterances were picked up from Leo Sayer's "You Make Me Feel Like Dancin.'" I wonder if I was the only kindergartner in history who took ABBA's album to school for show 'n' tell.

I would sing my heart out while performing very intricate, cutting-edge choreography to Donna Summer's "Dim All the Lights." I had a captive audience which consisted solely of my mother, until she would suddenly have to make an urgent phone call. I was undeterred; the show carried on without her.

If the rest of my family found me a little bit strange, I never caught on. However, I had a slight hunch I was different, always. I do not think the phrase "Bad Girls, Toot Toot Beep Beep" is all that common in the vernacular of most four-year-olds. I knew I had different interests than other little boys. Still, as I got older, I did try in my own way to conform.

It would be easy to point the finger at my father for my gender confusion. Easy, but unfair. Following my parents' divorce when I was six, we would spend Sundays with our dad. I looked forward to these Sundays because we usually went to the movies. He took us to see Raiders of the Lost Ark, which I was far too young to see at six years old (Nazi face melting: really, Dad?); The Dark Crystal, in which the terrifying Skeksis scarred me for life; and the previously mentioned Xanadu, a genius film about roller discos that helped mold me into the man I am today. However, on one Sunday when I was about eight, I was told I'd be going alone with Dad, just the two of us. "Come on, Jake. Grab your glove."

Immediately my stomach dropped. Oh God no, sports, I thought to myself. Now he'll see me rummaging through the garage, looking for that damn glove, knowing I have not been using it.

"Where are we going?"

"We are going to the ball field; you need some practice."

"YAY!" I said with such forced enthusiasm only a father in denial would believe it was authentic.

Thus began a run of joyless Sundays of my dad trying to make me the baseball-playing son he'd always wanted.

"Straighten your arm."

"Don't throw the bat."

"Visualize the ball."

It never worked; the only thing I visualized was the Nestle Crunch I had hidden in my dresser.

My dad and I have never been close. I know that this estrangement has affected every part of my life, but I am telling you here and now that it would not have made the slightest bit of difference in this aspect of my life. I gravitated towards "girl things" like a big gay moth to a fabulous fierce flame. Every Christmas morning, I'd bypass my own gifts and go right for my sisters'.

"What do you mean Barbie's Dream Bathroom isn't for me? I don't want that stupid truck!"

"Cooper, do you like Strawberry Shortcake?"

I heard the taunt from across the playground, from where my prime tormentor held court on the swing set. Oh shit, what am I supposed to say? I knew he wasn't talking about the dessert. He was referring to the noxiously scented line of dolls that was all the rage in the eighties. Aside from the titular red strumpet, there was Blueberry Muffin who had blue pigtails and wore a top hat, boy character Huckleberry Pie, Orange Blossom (she was the black doll), plus many more. They all smelled like someone threw up Skittles, and each came with their own pet sidekick. What was I supposed to say? Yes, I like Strawberry Shortcake, you monster. And yes, I really want one of my own. Even at seven I knew I couldn't admit that to my peers.

"Why?" I said suspiciously.

"Because you're such a girl, hahahaha!"

Some kids laughed; some kids told him to shut up. I just stood there, trying to figure out a way to get my own Strawberry Shortcake.

In my desperation not to be different, I even joined the soccer team; what a special kind of hell that was. Once in the fourth grade, after being forcefully coerced to play football at recess, I mistakenly scored a touchdown for the opposing team. Let me tell you something people, little boys don't let you live that down. These boys, who acted as if I'd broken into their homes and gunned down their entire family that day, did not want Cooper the Pooper Scooper on their soccer team. They froze me out. I was totally invisible, except to the coach, unfortunately.

"Why are you even here?" this man, a father no less, asked me point blank one day at practice.

"Good question, Coach," I thought to myself. "You think I want to be here? Well, think again, tubby! I'd much rather be at home giving Barbie a sweeping updo, but no, we don't live in that kind of world, do we, Coach? Way to nurture children, asshole."

"Cooper, get your head out of the clouds and hustle, damnit!" He screamed it. He screamed so hard he had some spittle hanging from the corner of his mouth. He cussed at me. I even heard some other kid say, "Whoa."

I was going to throw up. "Coach," I squeaked, "my stomach hurts, can I go to the bathroom?"

He looked at me, a child, with actual disgust, and snarled, "Yeah, go on, get." Something you would say to a stray dog.

I had to use the bathroom in the school cafeteria, which was about as far from the field as you could get. Somehow, I managed to hold it in until I got there. I didn't throw up, I sobbed. I hated being a boy.

I came out when I was twenty-two. I am now forty-five and I can honestly say that never, not once in my life, did I feel like a boy. But the summer I came out, the moment I shed all the layers of shame and lies and denial and announced to myself and to the world "I'm gay," a funny thing happened: I suddenly became a man.

*That is part of the beauty of all literature. You discover that your longings are universal longings, that you're not lonely and isolated from anyone. You belong.*

– F. Scott Fitzgerald

## Melissa Barnett ❖ Untitled

For me, coming out wasn't one event, one moment, one situation... It was a process. An evolution. It's easy to look back on key moments now and realize that these were the incremental steps taken towards the realization of who I was, and living a happy, authentic life, but at the time it they didn't feel like steps, more like a series of confused stumbles through an all-consuming feeling of being lost and alone in the dark.

I remember being six years old really well. I don't know why, because in many ways it was unremarkable, but 1988, my sixth year on the earth, is one that sticks out. I distinctly recall watching the Wimbledon ladies' singles final and seeing Steffi Graf for the first time. Young, pretty, blonde, and bouncy, with a backhand slice that wouldn't quit (it turns out I have a thing for blonde, athletic Germans — hello to the soon-to-be Mrs. Barnett). I was willing her to beat the scary, surly, bespectacled lady on the other side of the net. Except I kind of wasn't. I felt like I knew Martina Navratilova. She felt familiar. Safe. Comfortable somehow, alongside being absolutely terrifying. I mean, maybe I felt like I knew her because she'd won Wimbledon every year since I was in the womb and she had transcended tennis, so I'd literally been exposed to her since birth, but it felt like more than that. She didn't just feel familiar, she felt familial.

Like kin. I can't quite explain it now, so there was no way I could have begun to rationalize or explain it at five, going on six.

Then my birthday came, and my parents bought me a VHS of Kylie Minogue's "I Should Be So Lucky." I remember literally squealing, which I don't think is something I had done before that day and can say with certainty is not something I have done since. Kylie was a bouncy blonde I loved even more than Steffi Graf (fast forward to 1998 and this was definitely no longer the case!). I'm not saying that six-year-old me in any way had a crush or romantic feelings for either of them, but what I am saying is that I had, and still have, no idea who won the men's singles in 1988, and Kylie was 50% of a pop duo with some dude called Jason, and I found what I felt was his interference in her career borderline offensive.

Cut to secondary school and I found most male behavior outright offensive. This was about the time that boys somehow totally flipped and went from being our nice normal friends to complete and utter idiots overnight with no warning. One day we were just playing Pogs together, and they would, oh so kindly, let us join in playing footie with them for 10 minutes (hello, misogyny), and the next day they were trying to throw daddy longlegs in our hair and pick us up to put us into the school's giant waste bins. The worst part was that I was the only one who appeared to find objectionable. what turned out to be their attempts to impress the female population, I lamented to my mother that I failed to understand why my friends would be giddy and squealing as if they'd just been given a Kylie video whilst being pelted with insects and dumped in the industrial waste, and she assured me that one day I would catch up and see the boys the way my friends did and enjoy the attention. Spoiler alert: I didn't.

It wasn't long after that that I first kissed the girl of my dreams. In a literal sense. I literally had a dream in which I kissed a girl. I can honestly say that before that night I had never had a conscious thought about kissing a girl, and I had definitely never seen two women being intimate, so this was just my subconscious mind bringing my true nature to the fore.

I was euphoric and kept playing it over and over in my head as I got ready for school that morning. The subject of my dream was an actor in a show I used to watch religiously; the cast of characters in the ensemble was incredibly diverse in ways I can't disclose without giving away who this person is (which will go to the grave with me), but as I brushed my hair in the mirror I caught sight of the reflection of the show poster I had above my bed, and as I cast my eye over all of their faces it hit me like a wave that if I went to school and told my friends that I had dreamt of kissing any of the male faces I could see — in spite of their age or anything else that might make my apparent attraction to them peculiar — I might be gently ribbed and mocked for a while, but it would be okay. But somehow I knew that if I told them that the person I dreamt of kissing was one of the women, I wouldn't be ribbed or mocked. I would be shunned. I went from elation to shame.

From then on my days were consumed with fear that it was visible — whatever "it" was. That people could tell that I'd had these thoughts and feelings, so hiding and actively putting them off the scent became my modus operandi. I'd had some practice at this previously; I shared basically no interests with my peers, I played golf whilst they played netball, I was the only girl in my school who played the guitar, and I would rather have been listening to my parents' Dolly Parton and Joni Mitchell records than the Top 20 (I grew out of Kylie quite quickly). To save face and try to fit in, I invested in some Take That memorabilia and accessories, and picked Robbie at random as my favorite when it became clear that this is what one does when they are a fan of a boy band. But older now, with more at stake, and Take That having split, I needed fresh and convincing cover to hide the new weirdness. I liked guitars, motorcycles and rock'n'roll, so slightly rough-and-ready semi-bad boys seemed to be something that would track and be believable. I chose Brad Pitt and Jon Bon Jovi as the new objects of my faux affections. Jon Bon Jovi's initials came in very handy for when I discovered Jennifer Beals and wrote "I heart JB" all over my exercise books, and did you know that in very low light, with his long blond *Legends of the Fall* hair, if you squint hard enough, Brad Pitt looks very similar to Steffi Graf?

There came a day I thought my cover was blown. We had to use newspaper to create a template for a textiles project in school, and as fate would have it, the page I opened my paper to contained a sensationalized double-page spread about an impending same-sex kiss between two female soap characters, with a huge picture of the kiss front and center. I felt all the blood in my body rush to my face and flush my cheeks, and panic-induced adrenaline prevented any cognition or action. I was frozen. The boy next to me, sadly, was not. Animated, he pointed to the picture, and to me, laughing and calling me a lemon. My teacher then technically broke the law (see Thatcher's Section 28) by jumping to my aid. She calmly diffused the situation, asking the boy over and over again what was so funny about the picture, asking him for something more substantial than "because they're lemons, Miss" each time that was his reply, until he and the class stopped laughing, he admitted it wasn't funny, and looked as flushed and embarrassed as I did.

Naïve as I was, I didn't know that "lemon" was my school's slang for lesbian, but then sheltered little me didn't know the word "lesbian" either. We're talking pre-Ellen, pre-The Puppy Episode, pre- "Susan, I'm gay" over the Tannoy in LAX. So, as mortifying as being faced with this image in front of 20 of my peers was, it was also helpful. Although I didn't get as far as reading any of the article — I just hacked into the paper as quickly as I could and got on with the business of making my stupid tie-dye hat — so I still didn't really have any context for my feelings, I at least knew I wasn't alone in the world. At least one other person — the writer of the soap — had also thought about a girl kissing another girl, and there was at least one person on the planet who was prepared to defend it. So, thank you, Miss Hart.

It's a strange thing not having any language or vocabulary for something. All I knew was that I felt the same way about girls as my friends did about boys. (I should clarify, when I say girls, I actually mean women. I've never knowingly been attracted to anyone under the age of 24, even when I was 13.) After the salacious kiss that was splashed across the newspaper aired, I started to notice more lesbian characters cropping up on TV. Although they were never outright identified as such, it was all very much intimated and suggested, and it never ended well for them. Take Zoe Tate, for example, one of the characters featured in the paper; her story arc went as follows: sudden onset acute mental illness; became a stalker; was raped, fell pregnant by her rapist; had the baby; murdered her rapist; blew up her family estate in spite when it was swindled out from under her; swift exit, never to return. And that was a positive portrayal compared to most! The message from the media was that my life had one of three outcomes: murderer, murdered, or institutionalized. And I still didn't have the vocabulary for the thing that made it so. Then it happened.

I'd always watched Ellen's sitcom and I felt that same weird familial thing with her as I did with Martina Navratilova, except Ellen didn't terrify the life out of me. (I feel at this point I should say that I have had the distinct privilege and pleasure to spend a little bit of time in Martina's company and she was as gentle, sweet, and kind as can be, and not scary at all.) When I was 15 years old the hot blonde lady from *Jurassic Park* turned up in an episode, rocking a power suit. Ellen started getting weird around her the same way I felt weird around certain people, and eventually Susan told Ellen she was gay, and I had a word for it. I had vocabulary. Not only that, but Susan was a successful TV producer and Ellen owned a book shop. Neither of them needed to be institutionalized, and the show would have had to have taken an extremely dark turn for one of them to end up killing or being killed. Maybe I would be okay after all. When people say visibility matters, this is why. Years of self-torture, self-loathing, confusion, and outright fear remedied by an hour of TV.

Okay, maybe that's an idealistic and simplistic summary of events. There was still some grappling with my identity to do, the inevitable denial, the still trying to be straight by dating a drummer with long blond hair who bore a passing resemblance to Steffi Graf in low light if you squinted... But hearing the word "gay" and seeing — I hate this word, but — "normal" people gay at least gave me the sense that there was the possibility of community and, more importantly, it gave me a sense of hope.

I could write another three of these pieces about coming out to everyone else after coming out to myself; the slow creep out of the closet to my friends and peers; the cringeworthy coming out to my mother that involved a futon, *If These Walls Could Talk 2,* and a dodgy DVD remote whose skip button failure has left us both with residual trauma attached to Dido's track "Thank You"; my parents' year-long festival of outing we dubbed Outfest 2004 before there was an actual Outfest... But the fact of the matter is that I still have to come out regularly.

Compulsory heterosexuality does not appear to be going anywhere. I think I'm what Ellen would have jokingly labelled a chapstick lesbian. I consider myself a tomboy; I don't own a skirt, and my dress shoes are just flashier Vans than my everyday Vans, but conversely, I have long hair and wear hip-hugging jeans, so I'm not necessarily readable as gay and don't tick all of the boxes on the standardized stereotype test. That means that there is always, and I mean the assumption by strangers that I'm straight. If I make any reference to "my partner" or "my fiancée" during a conversation with a stranger their response always comes back with masculine pronouns or some incarnation of maleness. "What does he think about you doing x?" "What does your fella do?"

I've been out for 60% of my life, I'm proud of who I am, and I'm very proud of my partner of 13 years, so every time this happens I make the correction, but in doing so I am forced to come out again, and again, and again. It's 2022. Ellen came out in 1997. Civil Partnerships were introduced over here in the U.K. in 2005 and equal marriage has been enshrined in law since 2014, but it is still, 100% of the time, assumed that I have a husband-to-be, not a wife-to-be.

So, about coming out: it was tough. It took years. Years of deep dives, long talks, finding myself, finding community. And whilst the world remains entrenched in patriarchal hegemony and compulsory heterosexuality it will be an ongoing process. My dream is that with increased visibility, and continual challenges to the current societal norms surrounding sexuality and gender, eventually we will reach the point where no kid will ever have to wonder for a second who they are and what's going on with them, will never have to make an announcement or correction about whom they love, and someone will just once ask me about my spouse, not my husband, making an automatic allowance for the possibility that I have a wife. But until that day comes, I will continue coming out and will continue to be proud.

Kelli Newby ❖ Later

I was 41 the first and only time I Googled "How do I know if I'm gay?" Asking the question should have been answer enough — no one Googles "Am I gay?" unless the answer is *Yes, even if you don't want to be.* Google offered me basic checklists and hotlines for teens. It wasn't what I needed. *What if I've actually been out as bi since college but I didn't know what to do about it or how important it was? What if I have a husband? What if I have a kid? And a pretty good life?*

When Google said "coming out late in life" meant twenty-nine, I gave up on the Internet and turned to a Magic 8 Ball, certain the floating doodad of destiny would reveal my true identity. *Reply hazy,* it said. *Try again later.*

❃

I was lucky to live in a time and a place where I felt no shame or fear about my teenage crushes on women — especially Catherine Zeta-Jones — but I received no further instructions. When I did encounter bisexuality, it was presented as a phase — a straight person's titillating adventure (bi-curious) or a gay person's first step out of the closet (bi now, gay later!). I liked boys too much to be gay, so that meant my girl crushes were a salacious factoid best used for getting male attention.

I took this to the next level at college. It was the age of *Maxim Magazine*. Dorm posters and popular films assured me that there was nothing hotter than two hot women making out. At a party or a bar, I'd offer to kiss another interested girl in exchange for free drinks. I absolutely did not want the drinks. I thought I wanted the male attention. I definitely wanted the soft press of breasts against mine, the curve of a waist beneath my palm.

But when a woman who had previously dated men started dating a woman, I would be part of the chorus saying, "I guess she's gay now." And, depending on how short her hair was, we'd say, "I always suspected" or "I never saw that coming" or even "What a shame. She's such a pretty girl."

And I was such a pretty girl.

❊

Family, movies, books, friends, and magazines offered endless advice and encouragement for pursuing heterosexual feelings, and I was good at it. I loved having a crush and always had a boyfriend who was smart, cute, and nice. When one relationship fell apart, a new crush on a new cute boy got me into a new one almost immediately.

Until I met Kim in grad school. She was a pixie-sized scenic designer with a cherry-red bob and a tool belt. She wore thick black eyeliner every day, even during tech week. After meeting her at a party, I found every opportunity to walk through the scene shop hoping to see her. It took me a week to put it together — the heat in my cheeks when someone mentioned her name, taking the extra-long way to my office fueled by fantasies of "chance" encounters... I had a crush.

I realized, too, that it wasn't my first crush on a woman. It was just the first time I'd recognized it. I was the queen of crushes. How had I never noticed before? And what did I do about it?

※

Thankfully, Kim made the first move. We began a casual but meaningful relationship we both knew would end with the school year. It is cliché but also absolutely true when I say sex with her was an experience unlike any I'd ever had. I found just as much pleasure in touching her as I did in being touched. It was too fun and exciting to dive into the why.

One night, my mother overheard me on the phone with Kim. I watched her registering the telltale signs of new love in my sparkly eyes and giggles. Mom didn't say anything until later, as she was waxing my brows because doing so "opens up my eyes."

"There's not another boy already, is there?" she said, exasperated that I'd once again started a new relationship immediately after a breakup.

"It's not a boy," I blurted.

My mother smoothed a cloth strip over my brow bone with a firmness I didn't usually associate with her. She pulled. I didn't yelp. I was too distracted waiting for her reaction. She sighed. "Well, let's not tell anyone quite yet."

And my heart broke in a way I cannot quite put into words, but I can tell you how the edge of the toilet seat felt against the backs of my thighs, the angle of my chin tilted up by her light touch, the tweezers poised over my face so she could pluck the stray hairs the wax hadn't grabbed.

※

Soon, it didn't matter. Kim moved, and, almost immediately, I started dating the guy my parents had always wanted me to marry. A year later, he proposed. A year after that, I married a different guy, one who'd swept me off my feet with his absolute apathy about gender roles.

We did what you're supposed to do. We had a house. We had two dogs and a cat and a Honda. We had a baby. My friends, siblings, and cousins followed suit. Summers were filled with weddings and baby showers. I was very happy, and this was how things were supposed to go. Two people devoted until death do us part. My sexuality was a moot point. Ten years went by in a flash.

❋

"It does matter," a new friend told me when I came out to her over sushi. She was one of the only openly gay faculty members at the college where I taught. I'd wanted her to know she wasn't alone. I dipped my avocado rolls in soy sauce with great precision to hide my blush at the weirdness of not only coming out, but also being told it was more than interesting trivia about my past.

"More and more students are identifying as bi," she said. "They need role models."

"Everyone knows I'm married to a man." My husband and I were a public couple in our small community.

"You're bi. That's the point."

I remained unconvinced that I could claim a queer identity given the circumstances of my life. I'd encountered one too many conversations on book Twitter about a novel where a bi-identified character ends up in a heterosexual relationship. People would ask, was it really bi rep or yet another straight romance being given a dash of queerness for marketing and hipness? Wouldn't me coming out on campus involve the same ethical murk, because I was claiming a queer identity from a place of extreme privilege to appear cool to my students?

If anyone else had said these things about themselves to me, I would have responded passionately with "That's bullshit, and you know it." I never extended this kindness to myself.

However, I did want to help my students, so I looked for opportunities to come out to them; but what personal details were appropriate to share, given professionalism and the student/teacher power dynamic? When a coming-out essay landed on my desk, I'd write a long personal response, then erase everything about me and leave only an enthusiastic note about campus resources for LGBTQIA+ students.

Undeterred, my friend got me on the list for queer faculty and staff gatherings. I was afraid to go. I figured the others would think *How dare she come into this space? She's never been discriminated against, and she never will be.* Besides, I was ten years married. It didn't matter.

"Being queer is about more than who you're attracted to," she insisted. "It's about community and culture. You can be part of it without being in a queer relationship. You *should* be part of it."

❊

To prepare myself for the gathering, I did what any academic would do — research. Under my friend's guidance, I started an independent study in lesbian lit and film. I saw myself in the stories, but not how I'd expected. Over and over, the main character doesn't fit in with their family in a way neither the kid nor the family can verbalize. Sometimes it's a terrible conflict, but sometimes, it was a lot like my family — love punctuated with a joking "Maybe you were switched at birth?" I also began to understand the importance of queer role models, as each character found someone who helped them understand what was going on. I spent more and more time chatting with my friend about queerness.

Spurred by these discoveries, I finally found ways to come out to my students. Their expressions shifted when they knew they weren't alone in the room. They told me with great enthusiasm about queer YA novels and fan fiction they'd read. What if I'd had an adult to talk to at their age? What if I'd had these stories? Would I have listened to my own inner knowledge instead of parroting the either/or? What if I started listening now?

Thus my subtle, intellectual coming out proceeded gently and respectably. Almost unnoticeably. I experimented with labels, using "gay" for playful dives into humor. "Pansexual" conveyed my disregard for binaries. "Bisexual" was great for people who found "LGBTQ" overwhelming. "Queer" demonstrated my commitment to community and sidestepped that whole bi/pan debate.

Then, just like in a classic lesbian romance novel, a world-weary butch who'd given up on love sauntered into my life, and my nascent self-awareness exploded into a tumultuous coming out. We met doing theatre, and one hike, a few afternoon drives, and several shared Ani DiFranco songs later, we were deeply and miserably in love.

I was very honorable. The scarlet A on my chest stood for abstinence. We hugged a few times, brushed fingers occasionally, but mostly we engaged in long, meaningful gazes. A month into our non-affair, my dear one moved three hours away, and we didn't see each other again for a year and a half, didn't communicate for large chunks of that time. My marriage fell apart anyhow.

✺

During the chaos of my marriage's disintegration, I delved deeper into my lesbian literature review, searching for answers to my situation, but mostly finding tragic endings. Then I discovered lesbian memes on Instagram. It was a "bisexuals can't sit in chairs correctly" meme that did it. My phone slipped from my fingers and clunked on the floor as a lifetime of never sitting properly zipped through me like a collage at the end of a suspense film. Clue after clue after clue snapped into place. I'd had sex with a woman in grad school and had recently fallen in love with a female-bodied person, but never before the memes had I ever said, "Oh shit, am I gay??"

Suddenly queerness wasn't simply about sex and attraction. It was about how I moved through the world. How I occupied space. When I took a solo trip to New York, I decided on the train ride down that I would navigate the city as a queer person. I saw queerness everywhere. Not in the obvious things I'd always known how to spot, but in short fingernails, an enamel pin on a collar, a tattoo, a pop culture reference. In a certain kind of eye contact.

The shift reminded me of a moment in *Interview with the Vampire* when the newly vampirized protagonist is told to "look with [his] vampire eyes." The camera pans over the graveyard and the world comes to life — plants have an inner glow, statues move. Everything is more beautiful. So, imagine that, but with gay stuff. Imagine me striding through the city, marveling at everything, but most of all at myself.

I was a newborn baby gay, and the whole world had an inner glow.

❈

The confidence and magic I found in the city disappeared at home. There, it felt like someone had rewired the house I'd lived in my whole life, and I was constantly flipping switches expecting an overhead light to come on but finding myself in the dark. I couldn't even be sure I was in the same house.

My husband wanted answers.

I had no answers.

It was torture for both of us.

Eventually, we couldn't take it anymore. I moved in with my parents, where I couldn't help but turn my lesbian eyes to my childhood to seek out the key moment I'd missed, the one that would have diverted me from this path of disaster, the so-called "root" that I had somehow ignored. Photos provided this soccer team, that short haircut, that really intense female friendship from junior high.

I began to joke, *Why did no one tell me I was gay?*

I watched *The Babysitter's Club* reboot with my kiddo and realized my favorite babysitter, Kristy, is one hundred percent gay. I reread *The True Confessions of Charlotte Doyle* for the millionth time. It tells the story of a proper young Victorian woman who, on a sea voyage home, fresh from finishing school, ends up finding freedom in joining the crew, wearing pants, hacking her hair off with a knife during a storm, and going by Mr. Charlotte.

Gay.

My Anne Rice obsession.

So gay.

That Indigo Girls concert I attended in 1999? Why didn't anyone tell me?

❋

At first, I'd respond to my half-joke, half-rhetorical question with "There was no one there to tell me," but that's untrue. While, yes, there was no representation in the media when I was growing up, I spent a lot of time in theatre circles full of queer people and queer culture. I shared a house with a lesbian couple my sophomore year of college. (Why didn't *they* tell me???) Then, as part of revisiting my childhood, I found "Draculina," a story I wrote in fourth grade. It's a gender-swapped retelling of *Dracula* that has my wry voice, my comic timing, and two women who triumph over vampires — and vampirism — to be together in the end. It is, as they say on my favorite corner of Instagram, so fucking gay.

Someone was telling me I was gay the whole time. It was me.

I'd spent forty years of my life letting other people define what queerness was for me when I'd known the whole time. And I was still doing it. Even the search for The Moment I Should Have Known was an attempt to find a short answer where none existed. If my confusion arose out of trying to understand my multitudes in a world of "this or that," why did I think there would be a single origin? Queerness is a rebellion against traditional structures — bisexuality especially because it cannot exist alongside the either/or.

It turns out the Magic 8 Ball had nailed my true identity. Hazy. Trying again.

*Listen to the wind, it talks. Listen to the silence, it speaks. Listen to your heart, it knows.*

— Native American Proverb

## Micah James-Allen ❖ Pieces of Light

For a lot of people, coming out means announcing to the world, who they love or who they've become. Some think it means they will lose everything, or their lives will be over. When many people get ready to come out, they think they must have everything figured out. Hell, even I thought I had to have it all figured out! But I'm here to tell you that this isn't always the case. At least for me it wasn't anyway.

For the past year, I had to listen to a podcast by Brené Brown as part of a group I'm in at work. At the time I had no clue who she was, what she did, or what her words would end up doing for me. Nevertheless, I listened to the podcast so I could be prepared for the upcoming meetings. I can't say how many times I listened to this podcast; but what I can say is after about the second round, my mind was blown! And that's putting it lightly.

You see, up until now, I had allowed myself to get to a point where I had completely lost who I was. Actually, I gave up who I was to fit into an extremely small box of who I was supposed to be. I did this so that I could keep everything I had: friends, self-made family, reputation, a roof over my head at one point; the list goes on. But the thing I failed to realize was that I had already lost. I had lost because a majority of my friends and self-made family were all conditional; my reputation was not only conditional, but was also based on being a person who was far from my genuine self. The people that "loved" me, only did so when I met all the requirements on an endless checklist, even when these expectations drove me to depression, anxiety, self-harm, and even thoughts of suicide. But somehow it all seemed worth it. It was worth it ... right?

I was born and raised as one of Jehovah's Witnesses. You know, the people who come knocking on your door on an early Saturday morning, and don't celebrate a damn thing. Yeah them, that was me. I never had a birthday party growing up, or Christmas, or a weekend that wasn't filled with some activity with my congregation. That was my life until recently. Despite being intensely depressed, I thought things were about as good as they would or could get. My failed attempt to leave 10 years ago plunged me deeper into my religion. Because if I prayed more, read the Bible more, knocked on more doors, dressed the right way, I would attain true happiness. I would have genuine friends, and the approval of Jehovah. And for a while I thought I was happy, even when I was severely depressed, because I was doing everything right ... right? For a long time, I thought I was happy despite what this version of "happiness" cost me. But I honestly didn't know any better. Because I was always told that being my true self would end terribly. That for people who left the organization, lives ended up in despair. But thanks to a global pandemic, I realized that this was not only so far from the truth, but that this world actually did have so much to offer.

When Covid-19 got to the point where Zoom became the world's new way to interact, my life completely changed, but for the better. When our congregation meetings went virtual, this allowed me an opportunity I always wanted and desperately needed. It allowed me the distance I needed to step back and see my life and my religion from a completely different angle. At first, it started with not getting dressed up for the meetings anymore, then keeping the camera off and doing chores around the house or browsing the Internet while still somewhat listening. After a while I grew so tired of these meetings. I started to log in, keep the camera off, and set an alarm to wake me up when it was all over. It was after several months of doing this that I started to struggle with my old but familiar feelings of questioning my sexuality and gender. I started to really ask myself why I was still doing all this. None of these feelings were new to me, but I thought they had become a thing of the past, something I could tuck away. The only thing I was ever allowed to be was the straight girl I was born as. But this time was different. Not because I had feelings for another person, but because after listening to that podcast I had a desire to be more vulnerable; to be my whole, genuine, true self. Unfortunately, I had no idea how to do this, so my internal struggle of shoving the real me into the closet continued. But the closet was full, and the door was bursting at the seams.

I started to really struggle. I knew the only way I'd ever be able to come out was to leave my religion. This would come at a massive cost. Leaving meant I would be publicly shunned and completely cut off from anyone that was a Jehovah's Witness. Anyone that was a Witness wouldn't be able to talk to me anymore unless I came back. This was all I ever knew. It was my entire support system. As time went on, the desire to be myself became stronger than the desire to fit in. So I started drafting my letter to disassociate myself, and looking for support in the few people I allowed into my life while still being in. I got enough assurance from a couple of people to realize that I needed to be vulnerable, and I needed to take a chance. A really big, hard chance, in order to see that I really did have support. I just needed to take a leap, to find it.

On July 19, 2021, I sent my letter to my congregation's coordinator and then a letter to three friends explaining part of why I was leaving. After several attempts to reel me back in, my disassociation was announced July 21, 2021. The next day, I wrote a long post on Facebook, coming out and telling part of my story. To my surprise I found more support than I could have imagined. I first came out as questioning for my sexuality and gender. The reality is I knew in my heart who I was. I always did. But I needed to sit with everything for a while. I may have known who I was deep down inside, but spending my entire life in a highly controlling religion left me with a new, but expected, internal struggle. Every way I was trying to live my life now felt like I was doing something wrong. When I had attempted to leave 10 years ago, my religious beliefs still hadn't completely sunk in. Over those 10 years, I committed myself to those beliefs more than I ever did before. I tried dressing more feminine, doing as much and as many avenues of service as I could, prayed more, read the Bible more, but at the end of the day, nothing could change who I really was, because it's who I was supposed to be. It's who I was meant to be. I think that's why there was always a part of me that could never let those beliefs fully take over. They were instilled in my mind, but they never penetrated my heart!

It's been months now since I left, and I've made some pretty amazing friendships along the way. Words can't express how unbelievably grateful I am for those who have stepped up and become my new support system. They have helped me through a lot of really hard and bad days. I mainly identify now as being pansexual, or queer, but honestly, I've realized that labels don't matter to me all that much. I'm still in my process of coming out as transgender. But those who do know have been supportive. Like I said, you don't have to have everything figured out all at once. It's OK to give yourself the time you need and deserve to figure things out and come to terms with whoever you decide to be.

If you're in your journey of coming out and feel like you're alone, I promise you, you're not! There's an entire community of people you haven't discovered yet. My journey has included years of therapy. There's a huge stigma when it comes to taking care of our mental health, but this is so crucial, especially when coming out. Starting therapy years ago helped me to become the person I am today. It helped me get to a point where I'd be strong enough to handle what has and would come my way before and after coming out. You might not feel like therapy is for you now, and that's OK. But please, please, find some way to take care of your mental health in a way that works best for you.

Brené Brown's podcast "Dare to Lead" helped me realize the importance of being vulnerable, allowing myself to be uncomfortable, rather than shying away from hard things, and to choose "courage over comfort!"

My willingness to "step into the arena" and choose "courage over comfort" is what has allowed me to finally come out and be my authentic self. Coming out has been the beginning of a new life, one I'm really growing to love. I love the person I'm becoming, even though it's hard work. I can't promise you that it'll be easy. But I can say that even if it may not seem like it at first, it'll be worth it. There may have been many dark nights, but there have been countless beautiful sunrises.

My name is Micah James Allen. I have something to say and a story to tell! And this is just a small piece of my story.

Lauren Lackey ❖ Diary of a Spaghetti Girl

Our love story has been nothing short of incredible and completely crazy. Lys (my redneck version of Melissa) and I met on a job interview. She was part of the four-person team who hired me. The first time I laid eyes on that beautiful ginger was at the University of Texas Arlington at the College of Nursing, in an academic advisor group interview. I was very straight and very married (insert cringe here) at the time.

I had been jobless for about eight months and in a passionless marriage. Loved the guy, but the poorly hidden lesbian in me could never quite love him completely. At the time, I truly believed that the sort of love and passion I had desired all my life was unobtainable. The stuff of movies, I had convinced myself. Which is why after five years of dating, my ex and I decided to marry. I knew from the beginning that something was off, but went through with it against my better judgment. Fast forward a year and a half and our relationship had completely dissipated to a roommate/friendship situation.

On the day of my long-awaited job interview, I curled my hair and did my makeup from the dingy bathroom of the Neuro ICU waiting room at Harris Hospital in Fort Worth. My father had just had his third brain surgery to remove cancerous tumors in an attempt to prolong his life. At this point in my life, I was quite lost. I'm sure at this point you may be wondering why I felt the need to spill all of these personal details, but they are very much vital to the story. Before leaving for the interview, I got a quick moment with my dad post-recovery. He said to me, "I bet this one is it. This one is going to change your life." Boy, was he right.

After being offered the job, Lyssa and I became fast friends and work wives. We bonded immediately over our love of the same early 2000s indie/emo bands, and our mutual burning desire to travel the planet, meet new people, and experience new cultures. She was the most interesting and intriguing person I had ever met. I was completely infatuated. I would even catch myself staring at her while she trained me on various software programs and procedures. She would later admit to noticing this and feeling pretty good about herself.

After months of spending workdays together, starting a new workout plan together, having the weekly post-workout pitcher of PBR together, I started to notice that my feelings for Lys were turning into something more intense than friendship. I found myself dreading going home to my husband (cringe, again) and wanting nothing more than to stay with her. I had absolutely no idea if she felt the same.

One evening after a night of dancing and a good amount of liquid courage, I admitted to her that I wanted to kiss her. After a stunned moment, she gave me a small smile and I immediately seized the moment.

Ok, here comes the extra cheesy part ... Fireworks, heavenly bells, birds singing .... All of it. That one kiss completely spun my entire existence on its axis. Don't get me wrong, as a very open individual, I had experienced my fair share of lady kisses. It was not something foreign to me. But nothing had ever felt like this. I mean, nothing.

We both realized in that same moment that we had fallen in love with each other without having a clue that it had even been happening. It was terrifying and beautiful. From there, as you can imagine, things got tough. Though the feelings between us never wavered, we each went through quite a bit in the wake.

I ended my marriage. I lost friends. People I had loved (and I thought had loved me) for my entire life walked away from me. My mother stopped speaking to me. All along, I was watching melanoma slowly take my father from me. It was the most intense, emotional time of my life. I had finally found this life-altering love and was losing the most important person in my life, all at the same time.

Melissa's friends were extremely skeptical at first. Cautioning her against getting involved with a straight girl, that it never ends well. Especially a married one, at that.

I found myself, my TRUE self after 27 years, only to lose my father shortly after. But not before he gave me his complete blessing. I'll never forget the moment he grabbed my shoulders tighter than he ever had before and told me that he would never care whom I loved as long as they loved me back. He was such a badass guy.

Now that I have gotten the dramatics out, fast forward to almost eight years together, and four years married, and here we are. I wake up every single day next to the most incredible person I have ever had the pleasure of meeting. She's smart and gorgeous. She's determined and adventurous. She's my biggest supporter and my driving force. She's my best friend and still gives me all the tingles with just a look. She looks at me like I'm the greatest sight she's ever seen. Even after all this time. I'm honestly the luckiest human on the planet. Our love story is dramatic, incredible, filled with loss and love, and so much passion.

*You know the truth by the way it feels. – Anonymous*

### Kristen Loomer ❖ Out Story

How many of us were given the moniker "tomboy" as a child? We liked sports, the outdoors, He-Man, Matchbox cars, always wearing pants and tennis shoes. We didn't like bows in our hair, dresses, or dolls (besides Barbie in her 4-wheel lifted remote-control Jeep). We played almost exclusively with boys, invited them to our birthday parties, and had them over for slumber parties.

That was me, I was that tomboy. My best friend in the world when I was growing up was the boy who lived next door, and we did everything together. Our parents would joke that we would be married someday. Sorry, that wasn't going to happen, Mom and Dad.

I realized I was different from the girls in my 4th grade class when they were all telling each other which boy they "liked." I was confused — I was supposed to like a boy, as in, want to kiss him? Eww, gross! It made me think about who I want to kiss though, and to my surprise and deeper confusion, I realized I wanted to kiss the pretty and popular blue-eyed brunette girl in my class.

Whoa. I can't be like *that* if everyone else isn't, right? As we all know, nothing can be worse for a kid than to be considered different. That will surely get you made fun of and ostracized. I'd seen it happen to the girl who dressed a little strangely for our standards in 1987. That wasn't going to be me. So, I wore the Guess jeans, I styled my bangs, and I joined the boy-crush discussions to fit in. Fitting in worked through middle school and high school. I had friends in all crowds and was a basketball jock on the championship varsity team. I stayed busy with school, sports, and friends, yet part of me knew I wasn't truly happy being me. While I didn't act "un-teenage-like," by any means, I had deep struggles with body image and being what guys would want because there was a part of me, albeit a very suppressed one, that knew I didn't want that anyway. College was fine and I had a boyfriend, but I was also fairly sullen and withdrawn much of the time. Graduating and finding a job that I loved at a local animal shelter was the key to finding and accepting who I was. That was when I finally felt a weight coming off my shoulders (thank you to all those women in comfortable shoes!).

For the first time in my life, I was working alongside out, gay people, and my brain simply exploded. So, it was possible to be accepted, normal, and GAY at the same time?! There were a few very attractive women around my age who were part of our social group that developed over the first year I was working there, and the crushes followed. My first kiss with a woman happened after a night at the bar — she was a co-worker and while I knew she wasn't gay, she wanted me that night. My world was rocked for the first time ever and I wasn't looking back.

When I entered my first real relationship with a woman, I realized I was in love for the first time as well. I was so alive, excited, and eager to be out like many of my new friends were; however, I never jump blindly into life-altering things. I went to a co-worker who was out and married and asked him how he told his parents he was gay. This sage of a man smiled softly at me, put his hand on mine and said, "It's different for every family and you can always hope there will be love and hugs, but sometimes there are other reactions."

I contemplated this and said, "Oh. OK."

He continued, "The best advice I can give you is to not have any expectations." Those turned out to be powerful, wise words.

I sat down with my parents in their living room — me on the couch, them on their dueling recliners. I told them I had something to share and that there was no other way to say it other than I was in love with a woman and am gay. I waited for their reactions for a split second before my mother pounded her fists on the arms of the tan, lightly patterned chair, stood up, and exclaimed, "I just KNEW that place would do that to you!!" as she stormed out of the room.

I looked at my father, who looked a little stunned, yet calmly said to me, "From what I understand, you are born that way and it's part of how your brain is." I blinked several times taking that in and then told him he was right. He nodded and I nodded but no other words followed for a while. While my Pops is no scientist, I know he reads and is an avid news watcher, but knowing he paid attention to that information enough to say it aloud to me at a time like that was still astounding. I told him that I was in love and that this doesn't change who I am. He said OK and there I sat in the palpable, tension-laden dichotomy of one parent blaming my workplace for "making me" gay, all the while visibly and audibly angry at my coming out, and one who attempted pragmatism.

There wasn't much else that could be said at that time, but in the coming days and months, there was a delicate dance around the topic. No, they didn't want to meet my girlfriend. While I knew this was going to be a long haul toward acceptance, I also knew my parents loved me very much, so we would get there.

Months later, they met another woman I was dating and that was a baby step. Many years later, they attended my wedding where my father proudly walked me down the aisle. I know for certain that they love my wife with all their hearts. People can grow and they are capable of change. My parents are examples of that. Sometimes time and being who you are without apologies are key.

It takes an act of extreme courage to be your authentic self, but it will save your life. It takes an even greater act of bravery to come out to those you love and if you are lucky, it will save your family.

AVIEL McDERMOTT ❖ The Non-Euclidean Geometry of Closet Doors

I've grown to hate the narrative of coming-out stories. I might not be entitled to, I have never had a truly traumatic coming out and have mostly been very lucky in my queer experiences, but I still do. Part of it is that I can't tell mine because I don't have one coming-out story. I have come out to friends, families, acquaintances, co-workers, and others. I have come out as every single letter of the LGBTQ acronym plus some, at one point or another. I have come, and come out, and re-closeted, and come out again. I have even had to come out to myself over and over again in self-discovery, the most pleasant and least easy to talk about of all my outings. Having to have coming-out conversations with people in my life about being queer has been as delightful as a visit to the dentist. At best there's relief that nothing's wrong, but it's always a reminder of how vulnerable some of the most precious and necessary parts of you are. My hatred of coming out has grown slowly as I've been forced to do it again and again. A significant part of my hatred is weariness.

I came out as a lesbian in middle school with some painful conversations with my parents. Not painful because of them, but painful because I'd already been taught fear and shame around my difference. I came out as nonbinary later in high school and had to explain what it was half the time to come out. I was incredibly excited about being nonbinary and at first rushed into coming out like an overly excited dog. After discovering that no one was as excited as I was and running headfirst into the opposite of enthusiasm, I went back into the closet a little and came out slowly. I was queer and nonbinary, and those were they only certainties. I came out to my friends as aromantic after spectacularly lackluster dating experiences, but had to confront some other identities after falling for one of those friends. This friend is a cis man, leading me to unearth my bisexuality, demi-romanticism, and the more masculine side of my trans identity. Through every step of medical and legal transition I have had to come out, awkwardly avoiding detailing the specifics. I still have to come out.

I would be happy never to come out again. I would be happy for everyone simply to be knowledgeable on LGBTQ+ issues and casually pick up on my queerness through the many hints I drop, and never have to initiate a conversation about it or correct an assumption. I never liked awkwardness; and underpinning the awkwardness of every single one of my outings has been fear: from the nervous edge of worry when I think someone's going to be cool to the thicker dread of coming out to strangers or coworkers. I have never in my life enjoyed coming out, it has simply been a necessary evil to get to the better times: being out.

I actually delight in BEING out. I am a big fan of pride gear, gender nonconformity, casual queerness, and bright colors. I love my visibly trans body, ambiguous wardrobe, and loving, bi boyfriend. I have a large collection of pronoun pins and pride flags. I have run several different small LGBTQ+ groups over the years. Queerness is delightful. Ambiguity is more comfortable than a stark truth. Being open about who I am is a raw, vulnerable joy. Shedding shame to go out as a pack of loud queer friends is the emotional equivalent to gliding through cool water on a hot summer's day. It's one of those times to delight in being alive.

The most joyful times I have come out have been within blatantly queer circles, with people who have cheered my identities or shared their own similar ones. Fist bumps around gender fluidity, cheers around bisexuality, welcomes from being on the aromantic or asexual spectrum. These have felt nothing like the coming-out scenes in the movies or with cis, straight people or strangers. These have felt closer to pride. Not an explanation or confession or identity, but a celebration and welcoming of it. Not a forced celebration or a celebration that pushed boundaries, but small and sincere marks of togetherness, rejecting a world that expects us to be ashamed.

I don't think anyone should ever have to come out. It's not simply that I support anyone's right to be private or closeted in their queer identity, it's that the fact of coming out itself only exists because we are all assumed straight and cis to begin with. It's that the titular tearful, awkward conversations or shaky relief that make up the classic Coming Out are all predicated on queer fear. Humans should never have been assumed to have only existed one way to begin with. No LGBTQ+ person should ever have to fear for their jobs, housing, comfort, safety, love, or regard simply because of their LGBTQ+ identity.

I love casually mentioning my queerness, in-depth discussions of identity, new discoveries about myself, but I hate coming out. I never wanted to be in. I don't want the awkwardness around my identity, even if it is supportive, I want to live in a better world. I want the opportunity to simply be in our identities for every LGBTQ+ person. For now, one of the tools we have is coming out, even as clunky, fearful, and painful as it can be. On the other side of the outness is where I have found a life of joy.

*Sing your song*
*Dance your dance*
*Tell your story*
*I will listen and remember.*

*– Utah Phillips*

## Janet Campbell-Vincent ❖ Learning to Be Me

The beginning of this story may resonate with many others in the LGBTQIA+ community. I always felt that I was different, even when I was very young; however, I was raised as a fundamentalist Christian. Our family had attended the same physical church since I was born, and the other family units in the congregation were an extended family. Having friends outside of this congregation was restricted, as the church taught that others would just lead you astray. The threat of hell was a constant in our family and church life.

When I began to feel true attraction and sexual feelings towards other girls my age, it scared the living shit out of me and I wondered what was wrong with me. I didn't want to have these feelings and, for years, I suffered in silence. I tried to mimic what other girls said they were feeling towards boys: a fake it 'til you make it strategy with a fortress built up around me, trying to keep my actual desires locked away. I assumed my feelings would change as I got older.

The sermons at church continued to reinforce the negativity about homosexuality. During a church meeting they did a panel discussion about homosexuality. I was actually looking forward to it being discussed and wanted more information. Is there a loophole that I didn't know about? Maybe it would be okay under certain conditions? Instead, it was equated to pedophilia and murder and anyone with those desires, acted on or not, was going to hell. I was terrified. Between these fears and role expectations from family and church, when I was 19, I married a man from church, Omar, and was pregnant at 20. I absolutely loved being pregnant. I felt so connected to our daughter, Debra, and even more so once she was born. Having Debra taught me what real love felt like.

Debra was born in 1991 and Omar lost his job during that recession, and we moved in with my parents. I began attending the local college while Omar tried to find work. I discovered I really loved college and began having friends outside of the church. It opened up my mind and I began questioning everything in my life.

I met my gay bff, Sean, at college, purely by coincidence. We were about the same age, and he was openly and unapologetically gay. Sean was the first person I told about my feelings, and that I was infatuated with one of my female professors. She was intelligent, fun, sexy, and exuded confidence. I was smitten. I still think back to her and what an impact she had on my life even though we were friends. I recall speaking with her and kind of dancing around the subject of being really attracted to women, and she normalized my feelings. She was the first woman to say it was okay to feel attracted to other women and normal to act on that attraction. I'd already begun questioning God and not just in the context of my sexuality.

I'd felt that these feelings from such a young age that I had to have been born gay. If "God" made me to be gay, then how could he condemn me for being how he made me? What God would create me as I am only to condemn me to hell? I had struggled with this for so long that I just tossed the idea of God out the window and chose to believe it was just a construct for control. I didn't need the fear of hell hanging over my head to do what I believed in my heart to be right.

I began keeping a daily journal when I became pregnant with Debra. As I continued writing in my journal, I realized that I was writing about my coming out and my desires towards women. I began always keeping my journal with me. I wrote while alone at college and used my journal as a creative outlet for sexual fantasies and erotica. For safety, my journal was locked in my briefcase, which was locked in the trunk of my car, and the briefcase required two different codes.

At work, I had many coworkers who were LGBTQIA+. I didn't know how to meet lesbians and I still wasn't sure if that's where I belonged. My coworkers took me to a lesbian bar, and I was in awe. I was surrounded by all these people where I could be my authentic self and it felt amazing. I knew that I wanted to act on my feelings, and this gave me a relatively safe space to do so.

My work required travel and offered a lot of freedom to be away from my family. I didn't want to lie about who I was, but I wasn't sure that I could be with another woman. I wasn't going to blow up my life and lose my family and extended family if I didn't really belong with another woman.

At 25 years of age, I hooked up with a woman who'd recently broken up with her girlfriend. I told Omar that I had to travel for work and would be gone for the weekend. I spent that entire weekend exploring the wonders of lesbian sex. Although it was just sex, I knew that this was what I'd been missing, and not just on a sex level but on an emotionally connected level. We weren't in love with one another and that was fine. I learned that this was what I'd been missing and craving my entire life. Imagine the wonders of tasting chocolate for the first time in your life and your entire body and mind and senses light up! I could only imagine what it would be like if I was actually in love with my partner.

I knew there would be repercussions for my actions, and I've described this time in my life as feeling like I was sitting on a powder keg holding a lit match. I knew coming out would blow up my life, but I couldn't live as I had prior. I had suppressed my emotions and feelings for so long that there was no space for me anymore. If you do not have space for yourself in your life, how can you have space for anyone else? That included Debra whom I loved the most; but I needed to be authentic for her.

I didn't know how to begin discussing this with Omar. Now that I have this information, what do I do with it? Where do you begin unpacking all these feelings? He resolved that for me but not in a good way. He had figured out the locks on my briefcase and gained access to my journal without my knowledge, and he'd had me followed. After reading my journal, he made photocopies of it, including all the erotica, and passed out these copies at his work and church and tried to get my family to read them. My sister was the one who told me about it when he approached her with it. It was a massive breach of trust, and it says so much about who these individuals really are as "Christians."

I'd spoken to Omar long before having sex with a woman and he knew that I wasn't happy in our relationship. He always threatened that if I divorced him, he would take Debra and disappear down in Mexico, and I'd never see her again. He was born in Mexico, had family down there and his family certainly wouldn't help me find her. I never trusted that he wouldn't do that. I consulted with a lesbian divorce attorney regarding child custody. She told me that since my parents would not allow me to live there if I came out, I'd be forced to leave the primary residence of my own child, and Omar would gain primary custody. I'd tried to get Omar to move out of my parent's home, but he refused. Knowing I had to leave Debra was incredibly painful. The only consolation was that my parents would allow me to see her at any time and she'd be well cared for by them, as Omar was not a present father.

Things can sound logical, and you can think you can follow the path you've laid out, but living it is another story. With Omar shoving me out of the closet, I had to tell my parents. I asked my sister to go and pick up Debra to remove her from any immediate danger. I spoke with my parents and told them I was a lesbian. My dad said I was going to hell and that there was no hope for me and then physically turned his back to me. My mom said she was worried about HIV which I thought was really strange but at least she was talking. She did say that I couldn't live with them anymore and wanted to know if I had money for a hotel. I told her that I needed to get some things at the house but that I was concerned because Omar was there, and I was fearful of being near him. Omar had told me he wanted to hurt both the woman I slept with and my college professor. I had warned them and informed the local sheriff's office, but they couldn't do anything without evidence of that threat or an attempt on them. My parents were told about his threats to them and Debra. My parents' response was that he was justifiably angry. They said that I could come and get my things and they'd take care of Omar and ensure my safety.

While driving home I felt a crushing weight on me, with my world turning black. I had to pull over on the side of the freeway as I had a total meltdown. There was no going back, everything was out in the open and I'd never felt so exposed in my entire life. My life was blowing up in front of my eyes and I had no idea where I would land. I had no idea if Debra or the two women would even be safe. I was incredibly frightened, but I drove over to my parents' house and went in. Omar was there, eerily calm. We all sat down and talked, and I realized I couldn't do it. I wasn't emotionally ready to do it. I said I'd try again to make things work, and they wanted to believe it.

The next day, I went to college and met secretly with my instructor and apologized for getting her caught up in my drama. I told her I'd realized something really important — that there are times when others can control you physically, but they can never really know what you're thinking. My walls were back up and thicker than ever, but with an intent of getting away from them with minimum repercussions. My professor told me when I was ready to leave she would help me in whatever capacity she was able to, but that I needed a safety net.

People truly do believe what they wish to believe, and it was a strange feeling to be kind of out of the closet and yet not really. I did what the church and my family required of me. Omar wanted me to see another therapist, which was fine. I'd gained so much insight from therapy but it had been in the context of Christianity, even though I'd told that prior therapist that I believed I was a lesbian. Omar wanted to select my next therapist and I was understandably hesitant about going. Appointment day arrived and she sat me down and said, "Omar has some real issues, but you and I are going to find a way to get you away from him safely." We began making my exit plans.

I had separate finances and my own P.O. box for friends to write for support; those letters went directly into my safe deposit box. I had a girlfriend, M. on the side, including an entire backstory for her which included a boyfriend. We'd been together for about nine months, and she wanted commitment from me.

It was almost a year after initially coming out that Omar said he wanted us to go out to Starbucks. It was outside that Starbucks that he asked if M. was my girlfriend. I told him yes. He said, "Well, you know what you need to do." I answered, "Yes, I do." I really don't think Omar or my parents ever really thought I'd leave. I kissed Debra goodbye, told her that I loved her and would be here often to see her, but I couldn't stay there anymore. I was finally ready and wanted to give M. and me a real shot, so we moved in together.

Omar and I divorced with the knowledge that Debra would stay at my parents' house with Omar and I'd have access any time I wished. Shortly after I'd moved out, I asked Omar what would happen if Debra grew up to be gay. He replied, "It would kill me, but I'd have nothing to do with her." I never wanted her to go through what transpired with me. I knew that when Debra was 12 years old, the judge would go with what she wanted provided she understood her request. I just had to wait and let her know I loved her. Omar was gone most of her life after that point for work, and my parents and I raised Debra.

When Debra turned 12 I filed for primary custody. I thought things would move quickly but Omar kept delaying court dates, since he knew Debra's wishes were to live with me. Debra and I were frustrated by the court delays, but things never went to court.

On his mother's birthday, May 25, 2004, Omar was riding his Harley from work when a fully-loaded semi made a left turn in front of him. He was struck in the intersection and airlifted to a trauma center. I had just finished nursing school a month prior and understood the extent of his injuries and that he'd never recover. I never wished this upon him. However, karma can be a real bitch — I look back at all the various threats he made towards me, Debra, and others. He never regained consciousness and was pronounced brain dead on June 3, 2004.

I hope he has finally found peace. I know that Debra and I have.

## Geddes Fielder ❖ My Coming-Out Stories

It's funny to think of that time when I came out over 50 years ago. A lot has changed, and a lot has stayed the same. I actually came out more than once. At 15, in 1962, I timidly came out to my friends. I lost most of them, but kept one. I was OK but it taught me to keep quiet about myself for a while longer. My dad was in the Royal Air Force, so we travelled a lot and I had to change friends frequently anyway.

In 1971, at 23, I had to come out to my mother, my Italian Catholic mother. I had to because I was sent home to await judgement. Let me explain a little… I had been in the Women's Royal Air Force for close to seven years, and a friend had turned herself in for being gay with a letter about me in her pocket. It was illegal to be a lesbian in the WRAF, so I was investigated by the Air Force police whom we called snowdrops for the white hats they wore. That was an interesting experience, to say the least. Sergeant Proudfoot (what a name) was in charge of investigating me. I believe she took singular pleasure in her job. She ransacked my room and read all of my letters and poetry, taking most of it with her. She went through my photographs. Interviewed me for hours in a small room. It felt pretty grim. At the end of all the interviewing I was sent to visit a psychiatrist in London who would determine my sexuality for them. I had a great time in

London. Stayed with friends (who were, indeed, lesbians) and went to a club, famous at the time, called the Gateway. That was a good weekend. On Monday morning I visited the psychiatrist, who gave me a survey of sorts. In England at the time there was a magazine called It was for young girls and ran surveys. You always knew what answer they wanted. The survey I was given was like that, so I filled it out with a load of BS answers that I knew they wanted. I was given a letter to take back in the end to show the powers that be. On the way back to Camp (I was stationed in Uxbridge), I dropped the letter in a puddle so I could open it and read it. It said I was not a lesbian but easily led and young for my years. Mission accomplished. I finished out my time in the WRAF. I only had one week to go; I got an honorable discharge, but my references were suddenly less than stellar. I threw them out of the train window as I left. I had been an athlete for years, competing for the Air Force and at Olympic level, and I was always lauded. So now I'm less than worthy because I was under suspicion of being a dyke. Come on! As for my mum, she got over it. When she met my ex-wife, she said, "Oh well, at least this one's Catholic." Quite the movement for her. My siblings thought it was a cause célèbre to be different, and my father, who was on the council for Lincoln town, paraded his newfound knowledge as a way to show he was able to understand things better than other council members since he had a lesbian daughter. Glad to help, Dad!!!

My third and final coming out (I had been out for a long time) was when I had my daughter, Vita. My ex-wife was the bio mum. I was in the delivery room, cut the cord and thought What now? When you have a baby, you must be 100% proud of who you are, 100%. That kid becomes the most important thing in your life. She was made by an anonymous donor and her birth story was still different enough for me to vow to always be truthful with her about everything. I was made her legal mother and placed on her birth certificate when she was five months old. I was placed in the father category (felt a tad uncomfortable with that) and I am still on it today, even though the British Government denied her dual citizenship because I was neither the bio father nor the bio mother, even though I had a court decision stating that this little life would not have existed without me. Oh well, there is that discrimination again. My final coming out was when she was born. I was out (still am) at work. I'm a teacher in California so not the worst place, although I've had my moments. My daughter, at 22, knows who she is and where she is from. And I can now say I have two ex-wives, as opposed to beating about the bush regarding the relationships.

*Every great dream begins with a dreamer. Always remember, you have within you the strength, the patience and the passion to reach for the stars to change the world.*

– Harriet Tubman

## MILLIE ❖ Bridging the Path

I was married to a kind man over 14 years ago when I officially came out as a lesbian woman. It was as terrifying as it was cathartic. I had always been attracted to women. I struggled to feel comfortable in my own skin. Walking through the stark metal-covered locker walls of middle school, I would feel much more comfortable in tan corduroys, a "Sit On It" belt buckle, and white and green Adidas sneakers than anything considered "girly." I was freakishly strong and could beat all the boys at arm wrestling. I was adopted and terrified of disappointing my conservative Irish Catholic parents, who had given me a shot at an incredible life. So, I married my best guy friend, whom I thought my parents would approve of. He was kind, witty and hardworking. We enjoyed the outdoors and playing sports together, but something always felt incomplete. It is hard to find the words, but there was this secret that was so buried in me that I began to feel hollow.

Very few people in the small suburban, conservative New England town that I grew up in even got divorced. There weren't any gay role models to identify with who could validate the empty and shameful feelings that I knew and suffered and which I grew well versed in suppressing. There was no one to give me shelter from these feelings that I felt were exclusively mine.

One day in my thirties, after getting married and moving out West, I completely snapped. I could not suppress these feelings any more. I no longer wanted to be a stranger to myself. Hiding my deep inner feelings became exceptionally difficult. It was time to let the dam burst. I was experiencing a lot of anxiety surrounding "coming out." I was afraid my parents would never speak to me again. I was fearful of disappointing my children and husband. I would have to tell my parents, and his parents, and my children, and all our friends. My world was about to transition into a whole new scary uncharted path. Oh, this "coming out" was not going to be easy. It was literally choking me slowly. Hiding my sexuality was not fair to myself any longer. I was not being candid with anyone else either.

I had been taking my children to preschool to socialize with other children and to begin learning in the school environment. There was another mom whose children around the same age as mine attended the same school. The kids became close friends in their separate classrooms. The other mom and I started having the kids over after school for playdates. I thought she was very attractive. The get-togethers kept increasing until we were having playdates almost every day. The kids were having fun and so were we. I'm still not sure who wanted the playdates to happen more.

One day I got a call from her and she said, "I cannot stop thinking of you." My heart felt like it was going to bounce out of my chest and my hands started sweating. I hung up the phone. I then called her back and said, "I feel the same." Utter panic sank in as I began to feel that my dreams were becoming real. I remembered a few months back that a lesbian co-worker told me to pay attention to my dreams. Dreams can reveal some truths and can actually be more meaningful than our conscious thoughts. I finally let all the images of kissing a woman into my night's sleep.

The next day the playdate mom came over. My mom had shipped a box of plates packed with styrofoam peanuts. I opened the box and the peanuts fell onto the wood floor. We both bent down to pick them up and I remember one of us saying, "This isn't what I thought we would be doing on the floor today." I remember my parasympathetic nervous system kicking into full force. When her lips touched mine my hands trembled, my mouth became dry, and I started sweating as if I had just stepped out of a sauna or a hot yoga class. But at that same moment, I knew I was forever changed. I remember how soft and tender her lips felt. No more living in the in-between; this was my forever path forward. All those dark feelings from the past began to feel less opaque. I could breathe deeper and exhale longer. Our relationship lasted around two years. We have since moved on and have new partners today. It has been a learning path full of relationship twists. With each relationship you learn what can work and what absolutely can not. I know today I have finally found the one that completely connects all those small steps forward.

My parents still struggle with my sexuality. When I first told them, they said, "Don't do anything capricious." I remember the statement making me furious. Why would I be taking this harder path and putting my family through this if I thought it could be any different? I was finally being honest with myself and everyone. My parents have learned to acknowledge my sexuality, but still struggle. They would never want to lose me, so they try to be accepting. Their religious roots are so deeply integrated in their values and beliefs that they cause conflict. I am eternally grateful for the life and love they have given me. I hold no regrets.

In this journey of coming out I have also connected with my birth mom. It was two and a half years ago that we found each other through Ancestry DNA. She has been completely embracing of my sexuality. I told my birth mom that in order to understand me even better she needs to go see my favorite artist, Brandi Carlile, play a live show. She hung up the phone and bought six tickets for herself and her friends and husband in Hollywood, Florida, right before Covid-19 hit. She is now a huge fan.

The biggest hurdle to coming out was trying to maintain as normal a life for my children as I could. I did not want other kids to be judgmental or see them as different. I did not want them to feel that they had to hide who their mom truly was. I wanted them to know they were loved exactly the same as before. The children were able to openly express that they had a dad and a mom and that their mom had a partner, all of whom truly loved them. The kids were able to draw pictures of their family tree which revealed that their mom was with another woman. They were free to draw another stick-figured adult on their art piece that revealed more people who loved them. I cannot imagine telling a child that they shouldn't express that. I am incredibly grateful that they grew up in a state that allowed this. I couldn't imagine the feeling of isolation a family must endure if such expressions of feeling were forbidden. All those hollow, empty-bodied, collapsed feelings would just come back. I could not imagine a world where my children could not tell their teacher about the two people who got them ready for school each morning and the ones to whom they joyously came home each day.

By coming out, I felt an immense shift in my personal life.. Initially I had shifted from spending most weekends with heterosexual couples with kids, to feeling left out and isolated. My ex-husband would spend most weekends as usual with old friends and families. The kids would come back to me and share stories of barbecues, hikes and mountain trips with the friends I used to hang out with. I didn't fit that mold. I don't think I was necessarily rejected. I just didn't feel fully accepted. It became increasingly easier to hang out with new friends immersed in the gay community who could relate to my sexuality. It was a social transition. It was important for me to be surrounded by people who shared the same struggles. The new community I had engaged in became my home. I no longer had to agonize over my internal feelings. I knew I needed to feel connected with this community without abandoning the old life that tended to burden my spirit at times. I needed to be immersed in the life my children had formed and blend this with my new open discovery.

My soul needed to transition into a steady flow that was only begging to soften.

I am trying every day to understand and break down the barriers that continue to exist with living one's true life. It is a delicate balance to bridge these worlds. I feel at peace knowing that this balance can and needs to exist.

## Carlo Gomez-Arteaga ❖ Learning to Speak My Truth

It was the year 2000. I felt paralyzed sitting in a cold, dark, damp movie theater, with tears streaming down my face, incapable of uttering a single word. I had just finished watching the movie *Boys Don't Cry,* about a young man named Brandon Teena who was brutally murdered for daring to live and love as a transgender man in rural Nebraska. I came home that night shaken to the core. But the violence in the movie was not the only thing that stirred me. It was that I related to the feelings Brandon felt — the joy of being seen as a man, the excitement and elation of falling in love — and his ultimate goal — of being loved as a man. I was in a deep panic. Was this who I was?

My upbringing in a first-generation Mexican immigrant home on the Southside of Chicago was very controlled. People of color and immigrants were not welcomed in this segregated city. I remember my mother would tell me about how white people would stand guard ready to beat up Latinos or Blacks to prevent us from entering certain parts of the public parks on the south or east side of the city. In the 70s and 80s, Mexican Americans made up a small percentage of Chicago's population.

At home I was also very controlled. I was conditioned to respect authority or suffer the consequences. Often a slap to the butt or a strike with a shoe or belt was my Dad's response to my disrespectful behavior. As a kid I was often reprimanded for being too mischievous and (rough) with my sisters. And, for as long as I could remember, I hated wearing dresses. My mother would excuse it as my being too shy, that I was just trying to prevent my underwear from showing. My mother's interpretation might have been partially true, but wearing a dress felt uncomfortable and foreign to me. Instead, I gravitated toward clothes that felt good to wear: a crisp white t-shirt, soft shorts, blue jeans, my favorite Spiderman shirt, and gym shoes.

Additionally, the pressure to conform had consumed me. Not only did my family and community expect me to be a "good Catholic girl," but I was also constantly being compared to my twin sister. She was ultra-feminine and loved everything about being a girl: the color pink, ruffles, shiny patent leather shoes, and all the rest. It became a constant struggle for my mom to dress me. I would fight, fake illness, whatever I could do to NOT have to leave home wearing a dress. At the age of seven I declared to my mom, "God told me it was okay if I don't want to wear dresses. If I want to wear pants, it's okay, mami." Invoking God was my way of taking a stand. How could a Catholic mom say to God? My mother, although she did not understand, did see my struggle, and finally capitulated and let me dress how I wanted. And when I was eleven, she sewed me a brown and tan three-piece suit. That was one of the happiest moments of my childhood, because I felt affirmed. A few years later, she granted my wish to cut my hair short. From that moment, I was increasingly mistaken for a boy, and this too made me happy.

Though I excelled in sports, my elementary school was too poor to support such programs, where my self-esteem could have been strengthened. More and more I was teased for being too masculine. Boys would call me "He-Man" and laugh. Deep inside I was convinced it was jealousy of my natural abilities in sports. I was in heaven when my twin joked to me about how one of her friends told her, "Your brother is so cute." She responded, "What brother," laughing at the mistake. However, the newfound identity I was starting to experience didn't last long. And, though I enjoyed being mistaken for a boy, ultimately I learned to suppress those feelings and feel shame for them.

The pressure to be "female" was enormous and I didn't want to disappoint my parents, who in my eyes had sacrificed so much to come here to give us a better life. I also struggled with a very old-school and religious community. As the years passed, I withdrew more and more. There were fewer and fewer pictures of me. Eventually, I gave up and conformed. I began to self-isolate, and try not to draw attention. I didn't know anything else … until I entered high school.

I came out as queer in my late teens, first to myself, then to my twin while lying in bed late one night after studying for a college exam. I mustered the strength to tell her. First, asking to hold her hand, then confessing that for the longest time I had feelings not just for boys, but for girls, too. "I have fallen in love with a mutual friend," I declared. She listened and lovingly told me, "I don't understand, but I have always known you were different from me, and I love you nonetheless." That twin bond is strong to this day. She is still my biggest cheerleader. Years later, I would learn that my sister carried heavy emotional labor around my coming out and in advocating for me when other family members didn't understand me. I only thought that I was different because of whom I loved and wasn't aware of the full spectrum of gender identity and expression, or knowledge of that long history throughout many cultures. I became more comfortable with my queer identity in my twenties. I began to gravitate toward identifying as butch and reclaimed my masculine persona. I eventually moved to California to pursue a graduate degree and find queer community.

In 2007, I was 34 years old, sitting in my girlfriend's living room. Her sister had just been over for dinner with her transgender boyfriend. When they left, I awkwardly asked my girlfriend, "Would you ever date a trans guy?" I don't remember her answer, but my follow-up question was one I had been contemplating since that uncomfortable experience watching *Boys Don't Cry*: "What if I were trans?" She laughed because she didn't think I was serious. I felt disappointed and feared her rejection. This experience added to a deeply internalized shame. Instead of taking the risk of opening up, I hid deeper. I changed the subject quickly and didn't broach it again until many years later.

Over the next decade, as I denied who I was, both within myself and with everyone else in my life, I began struggling to wake up, to go to work, and to connect intimately with my partner. It was clear I was spiraling downward. My health was quickly declining, and I withdrew from the things that mattered to me. I was depressed; I began projecting and internalizing a sense of worthlessness. As an organizer, I've fought for the rights and better living conditions for those most at the margins. But internally I was ignoring my own needs. I was in survival mode, just getting through the uncomfortable moments that had become my life. I had spent years in therapy asking the wrong questions. As I struggled to heal from childhood and adult traumas, I never admitted my feelings around my gender. I was in my mid-thirties and deep inside, I knew I had to make drastic changes if I wanted to continue living.

Finally, in 2015, I was feeling exhausted and lonely. I was contemplating how things needed to change while I was working away from home, and I had finally had enough. After quitting my job, I came home to rehash the transgender conversation with my girlfriend. That day I finally came out to her as a transgender man. I knew I needed to do deeper work to reclaim my authentic self. I returned to therapy to work through my fears, the internalized shame, and my recent break-up.

While experiencing a whirlwind of changes, I started caring for anise swallowtail and gulf fritillary (passion) caterpillars I'd discovered while hiking. This was my attempt to save pollinators and calm my growing anxiety. I learned something about myself while caring for these caterpillars: a typical chrysalis can take six weeks or so to develop and emerge. In fact, some transform more slowly, undergoing a kind of dormancy for a year or more before emerging. When an anise swallowtail in my care emerged nearly two years after I thought it had dried up and died, I was astonished. It took longer to transform than the others, but it took as long as it needed, and it came out when it was ready. I remember saying, "They're kind of like me."

Despite my internalized shame and fear of losing friends and family, I came out as transgender to my siblings, my mom, extended relatives, friends, and work colleagues. During that time, I also experienced transphobia at a nonprofit organization, and lost my job because of it. I knew that the choice was clear. I was done struggling. I found my voice. I centered myself. By 2019, with newfound courage and clarity, I was even able to come out to my 87-year-old auntie. I recorded a video for her, in which I explained that I was transgender, what that meant, what pronouns and name I preferred and why. She got it! All the years of fear and heartache melted. I finally could express my needs and wishes, and could feel understood, heard, respected.

There is a long and rich history documenting the lives of transgendered and nonbinary people all over the world. I may not know all their stories, but I am so grateful for their struggle, strength, and victories. In 2019, I started a support group because there were no culturally appropriate spaces for Latinx trans men to get the nuanced support needed in our native language: Spanish. Grupo Apoyo Fénix in the San Francisco Bay Area is now mentoring and creating a sacred community with other Latinx trans men to share our struggles and resources and grow our networks of support. The group works with school districts and other entities to make sure we create welcoming spaces and positive role models for our trans youth. The work to heal is continuous, and I know that I am not alone.

*Diversity is having a seat at the table, inclusion is having a voice, and belonging is having that voice be heard.*

— Liz Fosslien

Lorelei Ciccone ❖ My Coming-Out Story

I recently watched a Netflix animated dinosaur series with my 11-year-old son. It was a cute show about tweens and their dino-adventures, and incorporated social structures and diversity. One of the scenes struck me: a female character courageously divulged her romantic feelings for another female character. I paused the show to express my joy for all of the queer kids who may be watching and observing their representation. I couldn't resist the urge to tell my son, who attends public schools where Pride month is celebrated and who has had several classmates and teammates with same-sex parents like him, how incredibly meaningful it is to see this representation in the media. For him, it is normalized. For me, such exposure will never be taken for granted. What a game-changer it would have been for my sense of self, had I seen such a portrayal when I was his age.

I grew up in a small town where seeing a familiar face at the grocery store was a regular occurrence. It was in the late 80s, during my middle school years, when I began to realize that I might be "that." A "homo." A "lesbian." I was mortified to be branded with any associated term. "Gay" was the easiest to digest, but at the time seemed to pertain only to men. Nevertheless, each of those labels dunked me into a sinful and embarrassing container of "ewww" ... yet the feelings that I dismissed and strived to repress were of the most pure form of affection that I had ever known. Beautiful, exciting, loving, passionate, encompassing, overwhelming, yet incredibly difficult for an adolescent to make sense of. I studied my teachers, coaches, and school counselors for the slightest sign of being accepting of the queer community ... not for the hope of being able to share with them (an unimaginable endeavor), but for the hope of knowing that SOMEONE I look up to could possibly believe that I am worthy of dignity, acceptance, happiness, and health. It was during this time my mom shared with me that AIDS was God's way of punishing gay people. I know now that it was her loyalty to the Catholic Church that was truly the detrimental disease of that statement.

It was an emotionally lonely time. I continued with my days knowing that I still had a whole life ahead of me to make and do what I choose ... once I was an adult. There was not a single soul whom I could invite into this confusing, shameful yearning. Sharing with friends or family was completely out of the question, as the perceived risk of rejection and breach of confidentiality was too mortifying to consider. I knew I was liked and loved by many, but this ... this could have changed that completely, I feared. I seem to recall a mantra during that era that kids could and should go to their parents for anything: any problem, anything we needed help with, any trouble we were in, any fearful or upsetting feelings we harbored — our parents would be there for us with love and support. I soon learned there were exceptions to this rule. When I first came out to my parents, I wanted to give a big "FUCK YOU!" to whoever preached that mantra.

It was now the early 90s: still pre-Ellen DeGeneres's infamous "I'M GAY" announcement in the microphone of the airport episode. In my parents' defense, I did not make such a proclamation, because I wasn't even certain which label belonged to me. I was clear on one thing, though: I wanted their understanding. I wanted them to understand me better than I understood myself. I was still completely under their control when I began sharing intimacy with a close friend, intimacy that was next level. I couldn't get enough of this girl, and my parents seemed onto me as I neglected my other friends. They questioned my choices and desire to be with her. My mom's intuition of the friendship having an unhealthy dynamic was accurate. However, I did not have the tools to navigate this secret relationship that included several layers of complexity and immaturity. I was desperate for my parents to understand and to help me feel that what I wanted wasn't wrong, weird, or gross. I wasn't flawed. My drunk-on-love and adolescent state of mind convinced me to give it a shot.

My first share was to my mom during the spring of my ninth-grade year. For some reason, I thought I had a greater chance with her. I mustered up the courage to shakingly tell her that so-and-so and I were more than friends, which was why I wanted to spend all of my time with her. I suppose it was more of a demand on my part for her to understand this and to let me do what I wanted, rather than a proclamation and request of "This is what I am ... please accept this part of me." I wasn't there yet.

"Does this mean that you two are 'lezzies'?" my mom asked with a tone of shock and disapproval. "EWW, Mom! No!" Such a label made my skin crawl. I thought to myself, "Who even says that?" But that question was beside the point. I instantly knew that I had made the greatest mistake of my life. She didn't have the maturity or capacity to understand this. To add to the horror, she rejected my plea to keep this from my dad. I guess I felt even more embarrassed and fearful of his rejection. She explained that it didn't work that way in their marriage ... that they share important things like this with one another. I understood but was terrified and wished I could have erased the entire interaction. My mom was meeting my dad for a social gathering at the neighbor's house, so we left it at that until the next day.

After a sleepless night, my parents sat me down for a talk. My strategy was to say as little as possible. From my perspective, the only words spoken needed to come from them. "It's OK." That's all. Just those two simple words. What happened instead felt more like a scolding than a question. "So WHAT's going on with you two??" my dad demanded. There was no seeking for understanding; only for a solution that would require terminating the relationship as I knew it. I can barely recall the words that managed to escape me. I'm pretty sure I repeated what I had told my mom the night before, with the added claim that I still liked boys. My struggle was clear, but my parents interpreted this exchange as me needing their help to stop my involvement with her. Their resolution included me being forbidden to have sleepovers or other unsupervised time with her. I was devastated, pissed, and afraid.

My parents didn't know what I needed. They misinterpreted me and wanted this to simply go away. Through my growth and perhaps my own parenting experiences, I understand now that they were there for me in the only way they knew how to be. They didn't know how to support THIS. After what amounted to a coming-out attempt on my part, I retreated and secretly vowed to never share anything meaningful with them until I was financially independent. I recognized my vengeful nature, but it was how I coped. As for my "more-than-friends" friend, we managed to sneak around under the cover of dating guys, although we got busted kissing a couple of times by some of our friends. She moved away at the end of the school year, and I was left with heartbreak and the fear of haunting rumors, or truths rather, flying around for my remaining three years of high school. Things stayed contained enough. I subconsciously tended to my wounds by means of periodic binge drinking and brief, unsatisfying relationships with guys. I knew that one day I would find my people and someone to be the recipient of my heart's pent-up love and care. I had hope.

That "one day" came towards the end of my senior year in high school. I became involved with an older woman who had an enviable experience being "out" and part of a lesbian community in our area. Things moved quickly, as they often do in lesbian relationships. I was also making up for lost time and jumped right in. She helped me see the deep love that my parents had for me, and within a few months, I sat my parents down and let them in again. I shared that this is what I had tried to tell them three years prior. I think my words were, "I'm gay, and if you want to be part of my life, you'll need to accept that." My demanding tone was indicative of residual resentment, but their response was favorable, and I was now embarking on an easier path with them and with myself.

The coming-out process is just that ... a process. It's not a one-off event. It repeats with each new person to whom you want to show your authentic self. After high school, I would chip away at the coming-out list that included my brothers, best friend, the rest of my friends, my teammates, extended family, and co-workers. The feelings of risk and consequence were unique with each relationship. My experience during my adolescent years shaped who I am today in ways that are both positive and challenging. I am grateful for my awareness and knowing that we are never alone as long as we have our *self*. My parents are amazing and have been incredibly welcoming of my partners over the years. I feel very blessed.

## Andy Vinh Nguyen ❖ Here

A child's mind is quite interesting; it knows not what is right or wrong, and it goes with however it feels. Likewise, as a child, I always knew that I had some sort of attraction towards men, never women, and thought it was considered normal for others as well. I had no concept of what sexuality was, or how attraction worked, and none of that mattered to me until reality hit, and labels were thrown around in a game of dodgeball. Tumbling along, I decided to hone the label of bisexual to play it safe. I had never really thought of coming out to people but through stereotypes, my femininity made them assume. In the first place, I had yet to know the concept of coming out either, as I thought I was considered normal within society. How sweet it was to sleep in peace with no thought of my identity or fear of hate. Through dreams and nightmares, one may call déja vu, and though some thoughts stay dreams, others can become an ugly reality. Despite that, I consider myself lucky as my sexuality has only put me at risk a total of six times, and all that came with it was trauma, or as some would say character development.

It was midday. I hardly remember the details, as I was twelve, but the one fact that vividly haunts my memories is the disappointment in his voice which dripped into the crevices of rocks, eroding my flesh. The exact words escape me. as I don't care to remember that moment, but I'd hardly call it "coming out." My dad had found images of men on my tablet which he decided to interrogate me about. "Your mom and I have been crying all night," he solemnly said, "this is disgusting, why would you like something like this?" I was shocked, I couldn't even mutter a word as my supposed haven crumbled faster than sandy loam slipping through my fingers. "Do you know how long I cried?" my mom wept. "Stop liking these things; it's not right." That night I hardly shed a tear, and though I'm not sure why my eyes dried at that moment, I knew with a heavy heart that my relationship with my parents would never be the same again.

Soon it began, a constant "subtle" bombardment of heteronormativity thrown onto me by my family. Suddenly I was unable to participate in things considered "feminine." No bright colors, no pink, purple, light blue, etc., don't cross your legs, no nail polish, keep your nails short along with your hair, and no skirts, dresses, or high heels. Anything foreign that I did was treated with mistrust and I can barely express myself around my parents to this day. Then my mom started jabbing at my wound with a barbed needle once she chucked the idea of me in the future. "I hope you'll have a wife and kids," she pressed at the dinner table. "Treat her well." Instantly I broke down as I couldn't live up to her expectations, and for years after, I drowned in guilt as I felt I couldn't repay them, that I couldn't do this one "little" thing just for them. Luckily, a beacon of hope shone from a sea of mist, when my dad came downstairs upon hearing the commotion, saying he didn't care what my sexuality was. Though it may seem harsh, it felt like I was finally able to find a place to dock. Yet the glimmer of hope turned out to be bait laid out by an angler fish lurking nearby.

My dad and I were coming home from repairing my phone's broken screen and he saw a rainbow sticker on the inside of my phone case from when I had participated in the *day of silence*. Panicking, I asked him not to tell my mom because I didn't want to disappoint her any more than I already had. And like a little shrimp falling for the lure, within seconds, eerie silence and darkness surrounded me.

"I'm disappointed too."

Selfish. It began to feel selfish just to want to be happy. My parents probably didn't realize, but they were severing ties with me as if we were tectonic plates on a divergent boundary. Even after working up some courage to be able to educate while breaking down as my mother pushed the idea of me starring in a hetero family, she still wasn't convinced. She pulled the classic, "It's just a phase, you're too young to know," despite her knowing she was attracted to men as a little girl. Ironic.

I've stood by what I believe to be a basic unspoken rule in the LGBTQ+ community: never out someone. It can be incredibly dangerous for the victim or at least put them in an awkward position, which I learned the hard way. A family friend found out about my sexuality and loudly announced how she wished she had a gay best friend. Putting the issues of that term aside, she said it in front of my dad who didn't say anything, but for the rest of the day, I stayed clear from him and kept to myself in fear of having another talk.

I truly began to shut myself away from adults after this last moment. Every time I'm in front of some other adult alone or without someone I'm close to, I freeze and do my best to reduce the amount of femininity I show. Desperate to avoid any sort of incoming discomfort, I tend to steer clear of parents of friends, and family friends. I always played it safe even after asking, "Are they ... okay with me?" I was at the pediatrician's office, where my new pediatrician suddenly asked out of nowhere if I had depression. Shocked, I didn't know how to answer as my eyes became blurry while water trickled down my cheeks. I stayed behind a bit after the general check-up with my brother, and that's when everything poured out. Every story about my parents was spilled out to the adult figure whom I trusted. Standing in front of me they consoled me, and for once I felt some sort of comfort in an adult's embrace. Soon after, they left to inform my dad about something which had escaped my attention while I re-centered myself.

"I love my boy no matter what."

That was what my dad said as soon as he came into the room, and to this day, those words make me cringe. After everything he had put me through, every part of me is blaring sirens to get out and not to trust the sugar-coated lies. Confused and feeling betrayed, I looked at the pediatrician with disbelief. "You told?" I can't recall the look on their face as I scooted away from my dad's arms trying to engulf me like an angler's jaw. Only my ears were of use when they replied, "Is that okay?" Stumped, I nodded a yes while admiring the floor where I stood.

It has been a while since my last incident, and though I'm trying to repair some rusting bridges between the plates, I know my boundaries and will refuse to respond when my identity is subtly brought to light. I now know that I don't owe them a child, that even with all eyes on me, where the majority of my family speaks behind my back, and a brother whose vocabulary has not changed despite my sexuality, I'm still here. It shows that I'm somewhat resilient, in the way that I had to take extra precautions, I'm still here.

Where my silence has turned to irritation for believing that I had to stay silent, that I had no say in my own future, I'm still here. Where my ears have heard enough of slurs, and I can't even say my own sexuality because of discomfort from bigots using it as an insult, I'm still here. I'm fine, I'm fine, I'm still here.

When my brother shouted the f-slur right in front of me without a care, leaving me to sleep in another room, I'm still here. Where parental love barely reaches past the bare minimum, I'm still here. Where the lack of love from blood has left a hole, I found that family is more than genes.

I'm still here.

*When all Americans are treated as equal, no matter who they are or whom they love, we are all more free.*

*— President Barack Obama, Speech on the Supreme Court Decision on Marriage Equality, June 26, 2015*

### Breelyn MacDonald ❖ Stages of Awakening

My coming-out experience came in stages: Stages that were more of a process of coming out to myself, acknowledging my true authentic self in terms of my sexuality, to not being scared of it, to finally embracing it and allowing myself to truly be me in whom I love. If I had to break it down to key moments in life that lead me to this point, I'd say there were about four stages.

I grew up a full-on tomboy, riding dirt bikes, climbing trees, playing cars, etc. with my best guy friend, who was like a brother figure to me. We watched *Knight Rider, Dukes of Hazard, The Hulk, Chips, The A-Team*. He taught me how to properly hawk loogies and pop wheelies and hit jumps on my BMX. I was not into dolls or makeup and the only thing that I liked about the Barbie my grandma got me was the Corvette that came with her. Gowns and tiaras were not my idea of playing dress-up, but my boy cousins' closet full of superhero costumes with swords and rocket launchers? Now you're talking! I was a tough little girl, and I loved it.

As I grew older and into my teens and was supposed to be into boys and giggling with my girlfriends about crushes we had, I stayed on the tomboy path — the whole ogling over boys just never really happened for me. I was so content and happy just hanging out with my girlfriends, I felt like, "Why would I want to bother with flirting with boys?" As I got older and into high school, the fact that I wasn't as into boys as my friends were was starting to stand out to me a bit more. I ended up dating an older guy for a bit because everyone thought he was so cool and cute and he was into me, so I figured that's just what you do then, right? I lost my virginity to him, which is a whole other topic in the sense of a) it never physically felt good or right, b) I was never into it, and c) the fact that all of that was very obvious to this so called "boyfriend," and yet he still pushed for it to happen and I let it because again, I thought that's what I was supposed to do. That particular pattern with this fella has had its own ramifications on my life, but that is another story. After I ended that unappealing and unsatisfying relationship, I was again that single friend that just wanted to hang out with my girlfriends but did not particularly enjoy their conversations about boys or any topic of sex with them. This was me for quite a while — the single friend.

*Stage 1 — Acknowledging It*

When I was about 19 years old, I lived with my best friend and it was great. She had a daughter whom I adored, and we felt like a family unit. It was a very close relationship and I found myself starting to feel a stronger connection that I didn't even really fully acknowledge for a while, but once I did, I started questioning myself and the feelings I was having. Why would I so look forward to her coming home from work? Why would I get a tingly feeling in my belly when she was physically close to me? What the heck was going on? I started writing these thoughts and questions down in my journal, but I wrote them in a very ambiguous way that was vague even to me. Although I was writing to myself, I was wording things in a way that wasn't truly honest. Looking back now, I realize that I was afraid to be honest with myself about it because subconsciously I didn't want to admit that I was actually having these feelings. I didn't want to actually write out the words "crush" or use her name — I didn't want to make any of it real, and to this day I'm not really sure why. I think I must have been afraid — afraid of what she might think; what my other friends might think; that it would change the way I was identified, or the way people would look at me. I just didn't feel sure enough in myself to allow myself to be open about it. I did however intentionally leave my journal out in hopes that this friend of mine would read it, which in retrospect tells me that in some way I did want her to know. It was my way of telling someone about these feelings I was having without actually having to tell anyone.

Life moved on — she moved south and I moved away to college, but we still only lived about two hours apart and I would go down to visit her and her daughter almost every weekend for a while. This continued for about a year or so until some of my college roommates (who were also from the same hometown and had known both of us for a long time) pretty much called me out on it one night. "I think you have a crush on her, why don't you just admit it?" one of them said to me. Of course, my reaction was to completely deny it and tell her that she was absurd for saying that — I actually was very defensive about it, but it sat with me and seemed to pry it out from my own inner thoughts. It got to the point where I was finally starting to allow myself to acknowledge these feelings to myself, not in ambiguous language anymore, but clear thoughts of its reality. I was still inwardly confused though because I was aware of the fact that I felt what I thought being in love was, but I was still not wanting anything physically sexual to take place — that still scared me and I was still in denial of any idea of anything physical. It was clear that I enjoyed being physically close to her, I would even get butterflies, but I still wasn't ready to cross that line of being sexually physical — it actually made me feel really uncomfortable, but again maybe I just wasn't ready for that yet.

It started to become too awkward to keep these feelings in when it was becoming more openly apparent to me. I wrote (and rewrote several times) a very long, very ambiguous letter to her with a lot of vague pronoun wording: "There's this *person* I have feelings for," "I don't want *them* to feel uncomfortable because of the way *they* make me feel," etc. I still couldn't muster up the courage to say "you" or even "her" until finally at the end of the letter I said, "If you haven't figured it out yet, I'm referring to you," and that was the hardest part of the entire letter to write. I sent it to her — an actual letter in the mail — and nervously waited for some kind of response. It was a turning point within myself — this was Stage 1 of my coming out, the first time that I was opening admitting feelings for another woman, and holy shit was that terrifying. Even though I felt safe with this person and I knew that she truly cared for me, I still felt so vulnerable and exposed and afraid that I would be viewed differently.

It took what felt like forever for her to respond, and when I saw her handwriting on a letter in the mailbox, my stomach dropped. I grabbed it and went straight to my room and shut the door. What a relief to read from her exactly what I needed to hear. "When I read your letter, to tell you the truth, I wasn't all that shocked. It was almost a relief to hear you finally say it, and I'm sure it was for you too." She went on to assure me that she didn't look at me differently, she wasn't freaked out by it, and it didn't change our friendship — she would always be there for me, and she thanked me for trusting her enough to tell her how I felt. A huge weight was lifted from me by just letting this out, not holding it in and processing it alone, and being affirmed and heard and held in a place of love. Relief. We are still best friends today and she will always hold a special place in my heart for the impact she's had on my life and who I am.

After that first step of admitting that I had a stronger attraction and connection to women than men, things were still very internalized and not necessarily open — really only to that one friend and vaguely, almost jokingly, to a very few others, which was awkward. I hadn't actually had any physical experiences or even flirted with any women. I hadn't even ever kissed a girl, so how could I even know if that was what I wanted? But then my Stage 2 came along and my mind was blown and it was 100% confirmed.

*Stage 2 — Confirmation*

I was just about to turn 23, I was going to college in a pretty remote area and worked at an animal sanctuary with mostly women who were there for the same reason. It was a very bonding work environment and we all spent a lot of time together. I felt a particularly strong connection with one of these girls, and she felt the same — we quickly became incredibly close friends. It was the first time that I had moved away without knowing a single person, so forming this friendship was really special and we spent most of our time together growing closer and closer. I really didn't even acknowledge any sort of attraction to her, we were just extremely close and I knew she felt the same and it was great — we had a blast together and a really strong connection. One summer night, she and I and two other girls that we worked with went on an overnight camping trip together. There was laughter and dancing around a campfire and a lot of cocktails. At some point later in the night the topic of being attracted to women came up and this friend of mine admitted that she has indeed found herself attracted to women and there was one in particular that she worked with who she would actually like to kiss. In my intoxicated influence of confidence, I matter of factly said, "Well I can guess who it is … It's me!" Which was confirmed by her with, "How did you know that?"

Nothing happened that night, but the drive back the next day was tense and when it was just us back at her house unpacking our stuff, she said that she thought I should go back to my place because it was too hard to be near me without acting on this new revelation. It was like there was electricity in the room and anytime we came within a few inches of each other it was hard to breath. I agreed to head home, but on the way out we both nervously confirmed, "We're good — everything is ok between us," while also looking at each other like "What is happening?" We both knew that the conversation that took place the night before was not a fleeting moment; we just weren't sure what to make of it or what to do next.

Two days later she came over to my house for dinner and to watch a movie. It went back and forth from feeling like nothing had happened that camping night, to still feeling this new electricity in the air and a sense of nervous excitement. Of course, the movie we watched was *Wild Things,* with the classic 1998 provocative women's kiss scene between Neve Campbell and Deise Richards (go figure). The tension between us was becoming almost unbearable, and finally in a moment of laughing and wrestling together on the couch we stopped and found ourselves face to face within inches. She simply looked me in the eyes and said, "Are you going to make the first move or do I have to?" There was an internal pause, like the calm before the storm, and in that brief moment I felt a sense of both peace and euphoria, and it felt more right than anything else I had ever experienced up to this point in my life. We kissed and my heart exploded! I felt like the grand finale of fireworks on the 4th of July was erupting in my stomach and chest. It was something that I had never experienced before, something that I honestly didn't even know could be so powerful, and it was absolutely amazing. It was like all at once everything clicked into place and there was no turning back on the confirmation that this was the missing link in all those years of wondering why I wasn't attracted to men. Everything about that night was so much better than what I had thought it would feel like to be this intimate with someone. The softness of everything — her skin, her lips, her breasts, her touch. It was a woman's touch. It felt vulnerable but safe and completely comfortable, and 100% right. I don't remember sleeping at all that night, I just laid next to her in complete awe and enraptured in what had just happened, thinking to myself, "So this is what it's supposed to feel like." Everything was confirmed within myself and I felt more complete than I ever had before.

This relationship was amazing, but also incredibly hard. We kept it a secret from our friends and the people where we worked (mostly because of her wanting it that way), which had its perks of being exciting, but also became confusing to me on where we actually stood. It was fun to steal kisses in secret, catch each other's eyes from across the room when no one was looking, or to brush extra close against one another in passing, knowing that it gave us both butterflies. All of this while leaving at the end of the day to go home and be with each other — we were "those roommates." There was an exciting anticipation to it, but over time I began to realize that my feelings were growing stronger in a direction that she was not going with me. It was one of the most amazing experiences to be with her, while it also became the most heartwrenching. Not only was it the first time falling in love, but also opening my heart to allow myself to love another woman in a way that I don't know if I ever would have been able to do so on my own. Honestly, if it wasn't for her initiation of the whole experience, I don't know how long it would have taken me to confirm my sexuality. It was undeniable now to inwardly acknowledge this to myself, but in a sense I still felt alone and not totally comfortable with the conviction of it because I hadn't really been able to be open about it. The fact that she didn't want to be open about what was going on with us, that she would tell me that I was a lesbian, but that she wasn't, made me still feel alone in being "out" and kind of messed with my head. It was hard to be "out" alone, even though I knew that truth within myself.

It took me a really long time to get over her — longer than I thought, and definitely longer than I wanted, but besides all of the heartache I am grateful for her and what she gave me, the space that she allowed me to safely explore and the door that she opened for me. The realization that I could truly love someone, and be loved back, just not in the conventional way that I had always thought I was supposed to. The acceptance within myself that this was all with another woman was truly freeing. She will always hold a special place in my heart for all of that, and for being a part of who I am today. She gave me the confirmation within myself to move forward on this path, and even though it was always a secret, it was a stepping stone on my path to Stage 3, where I found my person in life and love her openly and unashamed.

*Stage 3 — Loving Openly*

Stage 3 is really an accumulation of the ones before. It is the stage where I grew to be confident and unafraid of who I am and of my sexuality. I am proud of who I love and I don't feel the need to hide it. This stage involves the woman I love and am married to, and have openly been with for 17+ years.

We met when I was about 26 years old, working together at a restaurant in our hometown. We both grew up in the same small town in the foothills of the Sierra Nevada. Both doing the same stuff as kids with our respective best guy friend — we probably rode past each other at some point on our dirt bikes, yet somehow we didn't meet until after I returned from college. We became instant friends and once we inadvertently discovered that we both had had previous relationships with a woman, we bonded over that hardcore with late nights after work night swimming at the lake over beers. It was so refreshing and comforting to talk to someone else who had been in a relationship with a woman, both of which had been for the most part in secret. I was not alone, and we understood the nuances that came with similar situations, and the amazing difference we agreed on between being with a woman as opposed to a man. The story of us getting together with all of its own fireworks and butterflies, and how it flourished into what it is today is for another time, but in relation to my coming-out experience, she was another pivotal stage. She was my first relationship with a woman that I didn't need to hide — there was never an impulse from either of us to hide it from the world. We walked down streets holding hands, we shared kisses in public, we proudly introduced each other as "my girlfriend." These are the things that straight people don't think twice about when they are in a solid relationship, but they are a big deal when you've always felt you had to hide that part of you. To finally be with someone who was just as proud to be with you as you are with them. The fear of being "different" didn't matter anymore. I had found mutual love, and it was too true to hide.

*Stage 4 — Telling My Christian Grandparents*

There was only one final hurdle of my coming-out experience, and that was telling my very Christian grandparents, who up until this point had no clue that my path in life didn't involve a strong, handsome man, but rather a beautiful, soft woman. At this point, all of my younger cousins were married and finally, after about the 15th time my grandpa despairingly proclaimed that I just needed to find a good husband, I decided it was time to let them know the truth. This was actually the most literal "coming out" experience I had. At this stage in my life all of my friends and parents knew I was not into guys and I don't think any of them were surprised by the slow progression of me acknowledging it to myself or to them. They seemed to always know that I was gay and were just waiting for me to come out with it on my own timeframe; but my grandparents were still clueless. I wrote them a long letter explaining that I had found someone that I loved and who loved me back. I listed all the great attributes about this person and the ways in which we were so compatible and made each other happy, and then summed it up with, "and *her* name is..." They wrote back telling me that they could accept it, but that they couldn't affirm it in their lifestyle beliefs, which was fine with me — I was just happy that they knew, and that I didn't need to hide it from them anymore.

Over the years, as they were around us and saw us together, they grew more and more open to our relationship, especially my grandma who now acknowledges to me on the phone how happy she is that we have each other and that she thinks we make a great couple ... even though after 17 years in a relationship there still isn't a single photo of us together amongst the other photos on the fridge of my cousins and their spouses — oy. But they know my wife, they know me, they know that we love each other, they know that we are happy together. They know, and I am comfortable with that.

All these stages brought me to where I am today — I am thankful for it all. Life is a constant learning experience if we are open to it. I am incredibly grateful to my family and friends for their constant support along the way, even if some of it was uncomfortable. For the significant women in these stages of my life who helped me get to where I am today, for loving me in the way that I needed in pivotal moments of my life, and for allowing me to love them back in ways that I didn't know I could. And for my wife for loving all of me proudly and openly and giving me this incredible life that we share together. I am confident in who I love, I am 100% unashamed, and I am grateful for all the stages that got me to this point.

## Brian Bowles ❖ Marc with a C

When I first saw Marc, it wasn't a *West Side Story* where I was ready to climb fire escapes and abandon my family heritage for love. In that moment at Paradise Garage under the old concrete viaducts in Denver, a hot nightclub was pumping out music. Jimmy Sommerville was raising his voice to a soprano line asking for the "Smalltown Boy" who was gay to have a chance at love. Marc landed in my crosshairs as the song faded.

Marc was a Greek god! I'm not exaggerating. I saw the biceps of his arms contract and release as he lifted drinks up and down from the bar, laughing with the bartender. Then I walked over to order any drink possible with my new fake ID saying I was 23 at the ripe age of 17.

"Can I get a single malt scotch?" I said, because I knew my dad's drink of choice would make me look cool. (Before you start judging, I was turning up the sexiness to the highest volume it would go. *Dungeons and Dragons* had not prepared me for this moment. Is it a sixteen-sided die at this moment and how many hit points do I need?)

He stood there and adjusted himself to my presence. My sexy vibe threw him off.

"What's the weather like?" I asked. This isn't even me joking. Yup.

That was the best I had to offer.

"Uh ... have you been outside today?"

"Well, yes. It's nice but chilly outside. You know what I mean?" He replied with that smile that immediately disarmed me as he said, "I wouldn't recommend becoming a meteorologist, but I think I know exactly what you mean. Tell me your name and shake my hand while keeping eye contact."

"My name is Brian. I'm nice to meet you. I mean ... it's nice to meet you." Oh fuck! Okay, maybe I *am* Maria in this story. Damn it.

"Brian, eh? I'm Marc."

A bizarre pause filled the space, and Frank the Bartender interrupted our love story by asking, "Hey young man! When were you born?"

"November 1st, 1971." Damn. As it escaped my lips, I realized my name on the fake ID clearly said "David Saint Michael," with a different birthdate. (Only a Catholic boy would try to use a fake ID with a saint's name.)

Frank leaned over and looked at my ID. Then he grabbed the soda gun and filled up the glass, saying, "Here's the Coke you ordered," as he winked at me to let me know my secret was safe with him.

Marc then looked at me with his very kind blue eyes, saying, "Here's where you ask me some questions."

"Oh! Sorry. Umm .... How's it going?"

Marc replied, "It's going great. Keep your eyes on me so I know you're really interested."

"Okey dokey." WTF? I've got no game. None. Less than none!

"Well, I'm not really available to date right now, but use these steps when meeting a new fella. You'll be just fine, and you might run a comb through your hair."

"Thanks. Can I at least know your name?"

Marc replied, "Marc."

"Nice meeting you, Marc."

"Nice meeting you, Brady. You're getting better at this. Good eye contact."

I replied, "Thanks again, Marc. My name is actually Brian."

"Brian? With an 'I' or 'Y'?"

"With an 'I'".

"I dated a Brian a long time ago. He was a jerk."

"Let me break you of the Brian curse!"

Marc replied, "Enjoy your Coke with no scotch."

He left. I'd destroyed any chance to ever have Tony on my balcony singing musical tunes outside my window. I'd met a Marc, and tonight was not the night. Screw you, Bernstein! Where's the song for this moment? There are moments when even I hate musicals.

As luck would have it, I saw him again at a party of a fella named Rob. (By the way, if you're trying to avoid having a gay son, I hope you're noticing a pattern to the names. Duh, people!)

Marc saw me and smiled immediately, like you would if a girl you once dated who you wished had drowned that summer approached you at a party.

I said, "Hey Marc! Do you remember me?"

"Of course I do. How could I forget? Future meteorologist?"

"That's me. It's Brian."

Marc replied, "Oh, I remember," and then he turned away to stare at a hideous painting of a mountain meadow that suddenly captivated him.

I asked, "Was it with a 'I' or a 'Y'?"

"Huh?"

"Was your previous Brian an 'I' or a 'Y'?"

Marc turned around and looked right at me, and then he smiled. This was a real one though. It passed the boundary of social grace into something else. Curiosity?

"It doesn't really matter," Marc said, "because that's not what's happening here, Brian with an 'I.' Are you even of age?"

"It's November 17th. I have been 18 for 17 days. How old are you, wise old man?"

He replied, "28 years old. So, I guess that makes me your elder. But I don't date children. So, let's get this straight at the beginning. I'm happy to be a friend. That's all."

"You'll be my Mister Miyagi?"

Marc looked puzzled. Maybe Mister Miyagi was too old of a reference.

Marc replied, "I'll be your older friend that will do what I can to prepare you for the crazy world you're about to enter." He then reached out his hand, as if we needed to honor this contract somehow. I shook his hand in agreement, but I definitely crossed my toes hoping that Mister Miyagi would someday become my Tony, except the stocky brown-haired Greek god with the sweet baritone voice version.

After six months of working on our friendship and meeting him at the local park where sexy gay guys played volleyball on Saturdays, a tall man named Vincent had his eyes on me and kept touching my butt every time we crossed to the other side of the net. It was the third game, and I was the worst volleyball player they had on the field that day, but

Vincent was definitely interested. His bald head gleamed in the sun, and his eyes leered at me through the net. Every time I tried to avoid crossing the net with him, he would always move to get into my lane. As the middle of the third game invited the crossover, Vincent came for me with his 6'2" frame and placed both of his hands on my butt, saying, "I'd love to spike that ass."

Marc lifted the net and walled right up to him. Marc's 5'9" frame met Vincent's gargantuan and unreasonably sweaty body with Marc's arms flexed against the "EARTH DAY" t-shirt Marc had worn out many times over. The t-shirt had the planet with humpback whales swimming in a circle around a peace sign. Mark yelled loudly, "What the fuck is wrong with you? Get your hands off of him." Marc was bigger in stature than Vincent, and the argument immediately ended as it started. Marc then raised his hand to me, saying, "Come on, Brian. It's time to go." Maybe this was my *West Side Story,* and I'm definitely Maria.

We exited the field to climb into his dark green Volkswagen Jetta with a sunroof and drove away as Marc broke the silence. "My first Brian was with a Y." I had just become his second. That night would be our first date. I picked him up exactly at the time he asked, and we went to the movie *Henry: the Portrait of a Serial Killer* at the Mayan Movie Palace right near his home. (Again, don't judge. It worked. Popcorn plus scary movie equals good times!) Halfway through the movie, Marc placed his left hand on my right thigh. He didn't just let it rest there. He grabbed my leg in his and held it gently but with stability. After ten minutes, he whispered into my ear, "You can rest your right hand on mine if it feels right."

The gentle smell of his Fahrenheit cologne with a note of cedar and cinnamon hit my nostrils whenever he would move closer to me in that chair. I have never despised an arm rest more than I did in that moment.

"Brian, I'm HIV-positive."

I can't write the rest of what occurred that night. My eighteen years and six months had not prepared me for this moment. Marc was infected. He was sick. He had the plague, and I replayed every interaction I'd ever had with him to ensure no exposure had occurred. My immediate reaction felt wrong, but fear has a cadence that sometimes takes the higher chord, drowning out all of the others.

There was a fermata being held with each passing moment as the waves of his statement landed on shore many times until he broke the trance by saying, "Brian, do you understand how a person gets HIV?"

I didn't. I know many reading this will think of me as an uneducated idiot at that point, but gay sex still felt like drinking under age. I replied, "No."

He could tell the light in my eyes had dimmed, and that I was not able to hold this space with him. He walked me to my car and held my door for me. He went to kiss me, and I turned away.

HIV meant death to me, and I knew I would die too. But I wanted to do whatever I could to hasten that death. The next morning, Marc called me, and his baritone voice filled the speaker.

"Brian, please just listen. I understand if you don't think you can do this. I wouldn't blame you. I really wouldn't, but I need you to be honest with me."

"No Marc. I want to do this. I really do. I'm just not sure how to ..."

Marc replied, "It is my job to protect you. I won't allow you to do anything that places you at risk."

"How did you get this?" I asked.

"From the Brian with a Y."

That summer, Marc and I made out and held hands for many weeks. Then, one night, he was wearing that damn sexy Earth Day t-shirt. I knew I was ready. As I removed his t-shirt, his large torso and hairy chest revealed a strong and powerful man.

"Marc, why do you keep this old t-shirt that is barely holding together?"

"Brian, this t-shirt has been with me for a long time. It was given to me by a dear friend when I was first diagnosed with HIV."

"But why this t-shirt? It's just a shirt."

"You see an old, tattered shirt, but I see a reminder of how many days I have walked this Earth since the day I knew I was going to die."

Marc picked it back up and held it up. "How do humpback whales migrate across oceans every year to have their babies?"

"I have no clue."

"Exactly. You see an old shirt, but I see a map."

I replied, "A map?"

"A map doesn't always just tell you where you're going. It tells you how to get back home."

Okay, I get it. He's a bit Mister Miyagi if Mister Miyagi had been hot as hell.

That evening, Marc showed me how a man makes love to another man with no risk whatsoever. One might say we waxed on and then waxed off (terrible joke!).

Every first love must end. It crescendos in early August, as the afternoon breezes promise the return of winter's song.

"Brian, we need to be done," Marc said.

"What do you mean?" I said.

"You're going to college, and I'm ...," Marc said.

"We talked about this. Marc, don't ...," I pleaded.

"We are done. Things are not .... I have AIDS."

"No!"

"Yes, Brian. I'm officially below 200. I'm moving in with my dad. You must trust me."

I was getting ready to launch my life, and he was accepting the ending of his.

"Marc, come on. We can go through this together."

"Brian, we knew this had an end date. I love you."

The first time he said those words offered an ending.

In 1991, two years later, I would get a call in the fall of my sophomore year, and Marc's voice greeted me in the static. Marc asked, "Is this the Brian with an I?"

"Yes." That's all I could say.

"Brian, I don't have a lot of time, but you need you to know something." His energy swam across the phone lines, and he was in front of me with his blue eyes. He was right there, and any static temporarily vanished.

"Of course, Marc. I'm listening."

"Brian, I'm at the hospital in San Francisco. My dad is with me."

"You made it to California to be with your dad? That's great!" I ignored the word "hospital" completely. It had a different note, and my brain was tossing that one around waiting for it to land.

"Brian, I don't have long now."

"Marc, I ..."

Marc responded, "Brian, I'm sorry to drop this bomb. I need you to know I loved you. I mean, 'I love you.' I always have. My dad will be reaching out to you after ..."

I heard his tears fill the phone, and his dad grabbed the phone. "Marc needs to go. He needs his rest."

That was all. Three days later, his father left a voice message letting me know that his son Marc, my Marc, the only Marc with a "C" I'd ever known, had died that morning.

At that time, Death was final and unforgiving. I had met Death for the first time, and that bitch and I were not yet on speaking terms.

The package arrived from his dad two weeks later. That night, I felt very strongly that I needed to open the box that sat in the bottom of a closet wrapped in a duffel bag. There was a small envelope with my name written across: BRIAN WITH AN I. I thought it was a joke from Marc, but it turned out to be a letter from his dad. It was on basic white stationery and his father thanked me for loving his son. The idea of a father thanking me for loving his son was hard to imagine, and yet, this letter in three sentences offered the gentle words of a father from the heart of his gentle son.

As I opened it, the white perfectly folded t-shirt I had begged him to throw out emerged. The circle of blues and purples ran together. Then, the peace symbol emerged. I saw it fully for the first time. Marc was at peace. It had truly been a map.

I felt a peace beyond words wash over me as I held that t-shirt close to me. The smell of his Fahrenheit cologne greeted me, and I knew that he would always be with me.

*The courage it takes to share your story might be the very thing someone else needs to open their heart to hope.*

*— Unknown*

Nikki Lorton Krutzsch ❖ My Story

I'm about 1,900 words deep when my phone alerts me to a text. Anyone who knows me, knows I love Brandi Carlile. That voice brings me to my knees, and her lyrics are the story of my life. It's not uncommon for friends and acquaintances to tag me in all things Brandi on the socials. The video that came across my phone was a dance recital with a beautiful performance to "The Story." How timely, as I was currently experiencing major writer's block.

The Story. MY story. Hearing the song brought me back to the roots of my coming-out journey. I am not a fan of the cliché term "journey," but a better word eludes me. For me, coming out was not a single moment, but a series of unfolding events that took place over many transformative years.

THIS story isn't easy to tell, but it's important. I have yet to meet a person whose coming out has been a seamless transition. Brandi sings, "There is beauty in the struggle," and I must agree. If my words help just one, then the tears shed while replaying memories and contemplating words have been worth it.

July 2009: I loaded the last of the boxes on the truck, kissed my boys, gave the home we had built together one final look, and choked back the tears. After all, this was what I wanted, wasn't it? I had finally found the courage to own my truth and live in it.

From a young age, I was attracted to women, but also had feelings toward boys. I was infatuated with my female teachers and coaches, but also liked the attention the guys gave me. The teachers fed my need for affection, made me feel worthy of attention, and seemed to accept me just as I was. I wasn't girly. I loved sports, playing in the creek and woods, wearing parachute pants, and making my short, permed hair curl over my forehead like Michael Jackson's. Don't judge me. It was pre-Neverland.

As far as the boys went, I didn't particularly feel much toward them, but I did thrive on the attention they gave me. It wasn't like boys were knocking down the door of a teenage girl who looked more like Ken than Barbie, but I still managed to have a few *lucky* guys in my life. When I had boyfriends, more attention came from family and friends, and I craved that, however confusing it was. Wasn't this what "normal" girls wanted? The physical part was exciting, but the disgust and shame I felt afterwards was so confusing. Maybe it was because I was taught that sex outside of marriage was a sin and I was now dirty and used. When everything you hear and learn is laden with scriptures about the dangers of sex, it does the opposite of what was intended. It becomes all you can think about.

Most of my young life was spent under the teachings of a church steeped in Pentecostal traditions, and that laid the way too much guilt. On top of the teenage hormones and weird emotional pulls, the confusion was a real mind f*ck. Sorry. The ingrained church girl still cringes at herself for cursing, although those words tend to flow freely from time to time. My bad, God.

Unlike many I know who have left it, the church did not hurt me. In fact, I credit the church and the people in it for saving my parents' marriage, and consequently affording me the life I had despite the struggles some of its teachings brought me.

# My Story

In 1978, my parents built a house closer to my dad's work and we moved into a dreamy new neighborhood. The dreams quickly turned to nightmares. The financial stressors, coupled with my parents' selfish lifestyles, led to tumultuous moments in our home. On more than one occasion I became the protector of my younger sister and brother, and also of my mother. My dad was larger than life, and at times his physical presence and loud booming voice scared me. My parents' arguments turned physical, and I tried to help my mom. While small in stature, her will and mouth were mighty. That's usually what started the fighting, but there was no excuse for what she endured. When my mom cried out for help, my dad's words won. I could never help her the way she needed. To this day, I still feel the need to protect my 70-year-old strong-willed mother.

Our dear neighbors befriended our family. They were church people. That saved my mom and dad. We jumped into church, both my parents were saved, and our lives quickly took a U-turn. No longer were my parents living their old lives. They had devoted themselves to one another, and we now spent our weekends at home groups, Sunday school, and church. I am not candy coating this experience, but God saved my family. There is no doubt about it. I know there are skeptics and people who hate the church or don't believe in God. I suppose living it and experiencing the change in my family is what sticks with me. I saw my dad turn into a humble being with soft edges and a heart for people. My parents opened their homes to families in need, housing and feeding many, loaning cars to others, and serving where needed.

During this same time, my public school closed, and my parents opted to send us to the church school. It was here relationships with several teachers and coaches were forged, and I came into myself. While I was still struggling with my sexuality and not quite ever fitting in with the girls, sports gave me an outlet. I made a best friend and really loved all parts of high school.

My best friend, Paula, and I played softball, volleyball, and basketball together. We were co-editors of the yearbook, were student council members, and even had jobs at the same ice cream shop at the mall. My identity seemed to meld into hers. What Paula said and thought, whether I agreed with it or not, I took on as mine. I've often wondered why I wasn't strong enough to stand on my own back then, but I think I was emotionally stunted due to the trauma that had surrounded my household. I tried for so long to hide what I lived with that I became what people wanted me to be. That behavior easily continued into high school.

It was now the 1980s and homosexuality and AIDS were the headlines in the news. All I ever heard or read about gay people was tied to sin, disgust, and ultimately death. It was a lifestyle portrayed as perverted. Who would want to be associated with that? It was also during this time that I remember Paula hissing, "Eww, he's GAY!" toward a very stylishly dressed man who walked into that ice cream shop where we worked. My skin crawled at her judgment of this person we didn't even know, but I was intrigued. My interest piqued and I wanted to know more. However, living such a sheltered life years before internet access kept me ignorant.

Then college happened! I was away from home and learning to be my own person. I joined a sorority, made new friends, and began seeking out information that was now easily accessible. Paula didn't understand why I was losing interest in our old high school life. I wanted to branch out, and this ultimately led to the demise of our friendship. Freshman year also brought my first real crush: a girl who would later become my roommate and best friend. It was such a great time in my life!

Carey and I were drawn together during Pref Night, which is when you choose the sorority you want to join. Our conversation centered on Amy Grant and other Christian musicians. Wow! Here I was at this big school and had found a person with similar faith. During our three years together, we spent many weekends at each other's homes and summer breaks visiting one another. We were inseparable and I thought we always would be. During her senior year, as I knew she would soon be moving to graduate school, I told her how I felt. "I love you too, Nik," she responded. "NO! It's not like that. I feel different." She told me she would love me no matter how I felt, but she couldn't love me THAT way. It broke me. I had opened up my deepest emotions and shared so many scars with her. I felt vulnerable in a way I never had before, but now I was rejected. Things got really bad the last couple of weeks that semester. She graduated and moved back to her hometown, three hours from mine. We tried to let time heal the hurts between us, but our friendship would never recover. For the first time in my life, I wanted to die. The heartache was suffocating, and I thought I would never get over that loss. It was during this period that I vowed not to let myself get hurt like that again.

I broke that promise to myself, did what the Christian girl was supposed to do, and married Tim in 1994. Our first son was born just five months later. Now I was a young mother, married to a really sweet and caring man, but I still felt devoid of any joy and the connections I craved. I returned to my college journals and living in past memories in order to cope with my brokenness. In those memories I found comfort. One day, I found Tim reading my journals. I had been distant with him. I couldn't blame him for looking for answers. He questioned my relationships with any female friends. I think it was then that our mutual trust broke and would never recover during the next 15 years we were together. And again, I walled off trust.

In those coming years, I secretly found ways to connect with women. On more than one occasion, I ventured to the lesbian bar on my own, desperate to make some sort of connection. The internet also opened new doors, and instant messaging let me walk right into a new world. On December 27, 2004, I engaged in a conversation that would alter the rest of my life. What began as an innocent message with a coworker turned into a full-blown emotional and physical relationship. Amy and I are now happily married, but the road leading to marital bliss was neither smooth nor straight.

As I mentioned earlier, I have deep ties to the church. Shaking those teachings has been impossible. Coming to terms with who I am, who I love, and my faith has been the hardest part of coming out. During my marriage to Tim, I tried desperately to deny my feelings for women. I attended two Love Won Out weekend-long seminars, counseling groups for gay women, and individual counseling. One moment I felt strong and ready to commit wholly to my marriage, and another I was wanting to be with women. It was the hardest time of my life. I felt imprisoned at home, but now had two young boys who needed me. I wasn't strong enough to put my feelings aside for their good, and I regret to this day some of my choices. However, I don't regret being true to myself.

In 2008, amid Amy's and my on again-off again relationship, I attended an Exodus conference. If you have watched the Netflix documentary on Exodus, it paints the conference as a type of conversion therapy. Perhaps it was, but it was also here where I finally felt seen and known. The people leading the conference came out of gay lifestyles and were now living heteronormal lives. It gave me hope, even if it ended up being false. I returned home from the conference to my marriage and our children, dead set to make things work. Clearly, they didn't. Working in the same place and having the same circle of friends made separation nearly impossible for Amy and me. We lied to ourselves, thinking we could just be friends, but Amy was also wrestling with her sexuality. Knowing she was dating men truly gutted me.

I am not proud of how our marriage ended. The double life I lived for years hurt the people I loved most. The day I went to my parents' house to tell them I was leaving Tim was one of the hardest ever. Being the oldest child, I still wrestle with pleasing people. I knew this decision and failure would disappoint my family. But to come out, I had to break the rules. This led to years of estrangement with my family and friends. Paula and I haven't spoken since 2009. Her final words to me were, "You are breaking your family." She couldn't see that I was the broken one.

To come out, I had to endure heartache, confusion, loneliness, loss, and suicidal thoughts. It was a really long process, and I entered a deep depression. Sometimes, I wish I had just been able to rip off the Band-Aid back in college. But then would I have the life I have now? My sons, the job that led to meeting my wife, the relationships I made along the way, the support of my very best friends, and the love that found me were all part of my journey.

It has been thirteen years since I made that bold move to leave expectations put on me as a young girl and live my life authentically. After several years of wrestling with being out publicly, Amy and I committed our lives to one another in front of family and friends on June 8, 2013 and were legally married on the steps of the St. Louis City Courthouse on October 13, 2020. It was a beautiful day, smack-dab in the middle of a pandemic. Our wedding picture was dead center on the cover of St. Louis's major newspaper.

Ready or not, Nikki, here you are.

YOU were made to be loved. May you find the strength to embrace your own story and the peace to live in it.

## R.P. Chase ❖ The Beginning

The first shot was live, electric energy. It changed me in an instant. I tried, and failed, to describe the feeling to those around me.

"Like coming home," I told my partner.

"A relief," I told my friends.

"A veil lifted," I said to myself in the bathroom mirror. "A veil lifted." I repeated it. I couldn't get away from the cliché. This was supposed to be my experience, my story, and I couldn't come down enough to talk about it without my voice sounding far away, echoing, from across a canyon.

It did feel amazing. Like a rebirth, a final landing into the density of my adult body, and with it the full weight of almost 40 years of life. I had been asleep and now I was awake. I had been on automatic and now I was engaged. I had been static and now I had motion. I was embodied. I walked the full length of the house in my new vessel, my carcass. At 1,200 square feet, it wasn't that far, but I covered every inch. I was strong enough now with the shots to climb the walls too, and so I did. My first try was tentative — almost as a reflex, I reached out with my hand and felt the traction as my fingers connected with the paint. "Like a monkey," I thought with wonder, and up I went.

After a few months, I got brave enough to try the ceiling. This couldn't have made me immune to gravity. Physics was real, even if my 35 years of life to date had not been. And yet. I felt a warm pull, like a gentle shock. My hand hovered, and slowly made contact. One finger at a time, one toe at a time, I inched forward, until I was hanging and swaying in the afternoon light. The dust swirled, and I watched the upside-down cars crawl across the Golden Gate Bridge from my perch in the little house in the Richmond hills.

"Like a spider." I felt a little sheepish now, like I had a secret. The walls were one thing, but the ceiling must be a lie. Maybe a misunderstanding. I decided not to talk about it for a while, until I could say for sure that I knew how I did it. Or at least until I had a plausible theory. Not just shooting off the mouth.

It got a bit tense when people would come over. I had to make sure I did a sweep to get the footprints off the ceiling. My partner had to remember not to ask me for certain things ("Babe, can you reach that spider web in the corner?")

I had to find places to practice my new skills. Places where no one would be surprised, places where the wall-walking was normal, and it made you hot to hang on the ceiling. At the beginning, I could go days, weeks sometimes without even thinking about it. I would forget all about my secret life until I was back in my safe, secret spaces.

After a while, though, it got harder to forget. I felt an imperative to remember. I felt urges to climb the walls of the office, hang from the library rafters, and curl up on the ceiling of BART trains. Like a coming of age. But I was weary. I was grown. I had already lost friends and lovers, lost certainties, lost time. I was not in a rush to lose more. There's a pull to holding it off until the very last desperate minute, when your body forces the words out no matter the consequences. And I was determined to wait.

I started to see wall-walkers around more and more, though. Mostly they were camouflaged. Only visible to trained eyes. Things did not change for me until I finally realized that we were so hidden that most people could go their whole lives without even knowing about us if they really wanted to. And if we were really determined to hide.

I took it as a challenge. I tried hiding in plain sight. It sounded thrilling, but it wasn't. I was hiding from strangers' eyes. I was hiding from my future. I was hiding from myself. The risk to weigh was whether the unveiling would take more or less from me than the hiding. And no one could say for sure. I will tell you this — it is easy to waste away into the invisible, to forget how to see yourself, if no one else ever sees you.

But there was a lot to consider. If we all came out of hiding, would wall-walking be coöpted? If we all stayed hidden, would we eventually die out? If some of us came out of hiding, but it wasn't a critical mass, would we just suffer? Would I lose friends? Jobs? Passions? Places? Stories? My life?

The doubts crept in very slowly, in the form of pervasive, old, first beliefs. Dusty from being packed away, but strong. It's better to wait until it's safe. Hundreds of people have survived by carefully compartmentalizing their lived selves, their brilliance, and consigning it to the secret places. What if you're wrong about yourself? What if they are right about you? What if the phobic masses are right to be scared of wall-walking? It's a descent into the dark places. It's a conscription into oblivion. It's all in your head. It's all been a fantastical dream. It's better to get back to your real life and forget about this tangent — this awkward, sinful, perverse, deadly sidetrack to a righteous life.

These beliefs loudly asserted themselves inside my head, close to my core. They were nasty. They felt and smelled and tasted like lies. The alternative was a huge void of unknown. And that's the thing about invention and self-discovery — the handbook has not been written. You jump into the void and hope for the best. But whatever you discover, you know you will be jumping away from the lies.

This is coming out. Wall-walking in plain sight.

I wrote a "he-mail" to 250 people two days before my wedding. The bandage was easier to rip off that way — I couldn't have 200 separate phone conversations about my identity and pronouns. It's different for everyone. But also, the same. The revealing of a tender, painful superpower with endless potential for transformation. The opening of yourself to heartbreak. The first step on a path toward a more whole life.

And I am grateful to myself for taking that step.

This story is dedicated to wall-walkers everywhere.

# Acknowledgements

As a first time publisher and author, I am beyond grateful to a multitude of people for being a part of helping bring this important book to light. This book wouldn't be what it is without the medley of folks below who lent their help and positive vibes in the process of bringing Open Air Press Publishing Company and *Coming Out Together: Memoirs on the LGBTQ+ Experience* to blossom. Thank you.

**Family, Friends & Friends Who Have Always Been Like Family (you know who you are)** — for supporting me from the get-go in creating Open Air Press and jumping in with no idea what the heck I was getting into. Whether via an uplifting word, sharing news and updates, contributing donations or items to help us raise the capital, telling people in your life about the book, and just helping keep the trajectory moving forward.

**Lawrence Tjernell of Longship Press** — for guiding me and being a mentor of sorts as I set out on this publishing adventure. Your input and knowledge were invaluable.

**LGBTQ+ Centers across the country** — for all the work you do on the ground level to help marginalized LGBTQ+ people to have a sense of belonging. And to many of you for all the support and sharing of our cause and mission to your communities.

**Sara Bareilles** — for blessing us with the use of the lyrics to your beautiful song "Brave" that you wrote for a friend who was struggling with the process of coming out. And for just being an all-around brilliant, hilarious, compassionate, f**king superstar in this world (felt like you'd appreciate the F-bomb). I don't know you, but I adore you.

**Joe Biel of Microcosm Publishing** — for writing and publishing what became my definitive guide during this journey, *A People's Guide to Publishing*, and for your candid advice and help.

**To the podcasts and newspapers** that interviewed us and helped get the word around Open Air Press and the book out into the world and into people's consciousness.

**All the random, amazing people I met along the way who let me ramble on about my excitement for the book, the process, and my hopes and mission around it.** Sometimes it's those you don't know that you happen to randomly be sitting next to on some idle day that give the most needed and honest advice and feedback.

## Coming Out Is a Personal Journey

This is for those who, for whatever valid reason, aren't ready to make the very personal choice to come out.

The decision to come out should be yours alone. Everyone's personal journey around this is different, and there is absolutely no shame in not being ready. Only you can know within yourself when the time is right, and while it can feel overwhelming and scary, and your knees and voice may shake, please know when you do decide to crash through those closet doors, community and support are waiting on the other side to embrace and accept you for all that you are.

And if you decide that you're not ready, that's okay too. There are many different paths to living your authentic self, and while it might not be clear to you yet, there is support out there, and you are not alone.

— Shannon Ronan

# LGBTQ+ Suicide Prevention Resources

**National Suicide Prevention Lifeline**
1-800-273-TALK (8255)
Veterans: Press 1

**Text TALK to 741741**
Text with a trained counselor from The Crisis Text Line for free, 24/7

**The Trevor Project**
TrevorLifeline: Available 24/7 at 1-866-488-7386
TrevorText: Text TREVOR to 1-202-304-1200
TrevorChat: Via thetrevorproject.org

**Trans Lifeline**
Support for transgender people, by transgender people
1-877-565-8860

**SAGE LGBT Elder Hotline**
Peer support and local resources, for older adults
1-888-234-SAGE

**The LGBT National Hotline**
Peer support and local resources, for all ages
1-888-843-4564

## Open Air Press Is a Publishing Company with a Purpose

Our mission is to amplify marginalized voices in our society with the goals to:

**ILLUMINATE | RELEASE | TRANSFORM | PROGRESS**

In addition, Open Air Press will be contributing a portion of book sales proceeds from this book to the Looking Out Foundation, as well as the Matthew Shepard Foundation, for the sake of helping them further their important work.

# Notes

# Notes